Designs for an Anthropology of the Contemporary

A JOHN HOPE FRANKLIN CENTER BOOK

DESIGNS

FOR AN

ANTHROPOLOGY

OF THE

CONTEMPORARY

Paul Rabinow
and
George E. Marcus
with
James D. Faubion
and
Tobias Rees

DUKE

UNIVERSITY

PRESS

Durham & London

2008

Printed in the
United States of America
on acid-free paper ∞

Designed by Jennifer Hill
Typeset in C & C Galliard
by Achorn International

*Library of Congress
Cataloging-in-Publication
Data appear on the
last printed page of this book.*

To
Mary Murrell
and her dedication
to the past,
the present,
and the future
of the book

CONTENTS

1 Introduction by Tobias Rees

13 Dialogue I: Anthropology in Motion

33 Dialogue II: After *Writing Culture*

45 Dialogue III: Anthropology Today

55 Dialogue IV: The Anthropology of the Contemporary

73 Dialogue V: In Search of (New) Norms and Forms

93 Dialogue VI: Of Timing and Texts

105 Dialogue VII: Designs for an Anthropology of the Contemporary

115 Afterword by Tobias Rees

123 Notes

135 Index

INTRODUCTION   TODAY, WHAT IS ANTHROPOLOGY?

Tobias Rees

> Only by laying bare and solving substantive problems have sciences been established and their methods developed. Purely epistemological and methodological reflections have never played a crucial role in such developments. Such discussions can become important for the enterprise of science only when, as a result of considerable shifts of the viewpoints from which a datum becomes the object of analysis, the idea emerges that the new viewpoints also require a revision of the *logical* forms in which the enterprise has heretofore operated, and when, accordingly, uncertainty about the nature of one's work arises. This situation is unambiguously the case at present.—**Max Weber**

The background of the dialogues that follow—and of the questions discussed in them—is my own curiosity, which arose in the mid-1990s, when I was an anthropology and philosophy student in Germany. In the Department of Anthropology in Tübingen we learned about and intensively studied the history of ethnography. Our professors provided us with a raw schema of that history, organized in the form of paradigmatic works in their chronological succession, and encouraged us to read the primary sources. And we did. In lectures, seminars, and reading groups we followed the various ways anthropology developed. The story we encountered was—on the level of concepts and methods—full of ruptures. And yet it was—on the level of the theme around which it evolved—a most coherent one: anthropology was the science of the far-away other, of the "premodern," the "primitive." We moved from various forms of evolutionism, such as the work of Edward Burnett Tylor, Louis Henry Morgan, or James Frazer, to Franz Boas's historical particularism and the social ontology of Durkheimian sociology. Next we followed Bronislaw Malinowski's invention of ethnography as a social science and studied in detail the difference between his functionalism and A. R. Radcliffe-Brown's structural-functionalism, which inspired E. E. Evans-Pritchard and Meyer Fortes, who dominated British anthropology up until the 1960s. We turned toward culture and personality, got obsessed with the intellectualist approach of Claude Lévi-Strauss's structuralism, and fell in love with interpretative and symbolic anthropology in the work of Clifford Geertz, Victor Turner, and Marshall Sahlins. And finally, along with the critique of anthropology's involvement in colonialism and the emergence of dialogic—or polyphonic—ethnographies, we read *Writing Culture: The Poetics and Politics of Ethnography*.[1]

Writing Culture occupied a fascinating and yet a strangely odd place in that history of anthropology. It was fascinating in the ways it continued the history of the discipline, specifically in that it intellectualized—both analytically and politically—its key defining practice, namely fieldwork. It was fascinating as well because it opened up what was at times the rather dry prose of ethnographic writing to literary freedom. Ethnographers, beyond anything else, were writers. *Writing Culture* was odd, however, because it seemed to bring this fabulous history of anthropology to an end. It seemed to do so, epistemologically speaking, in showing that the premodern was less found than constructed (by the rhetorical conventions of a particular genre of writing, *ethnography*), and so it put the whole undertaking of anthropology, its methods, its concepts, even its object, radically in question. Within our scheme, therefore, *Writing Culture* appeared as a logical end point, almost as the telos of a long and complicated story.

What, I wondered, could come after *Writing Culture*? Were there any new developments? What did those new research agendas, theories, and approaches look like? What new kinds of studies were undertaken? It was clear that the "after" was an open space, but what this openness could possibly look like was far from clear.

To understand the event *Writing Culture* was—and the departure it stands for—it is helpful to go back in time and to highlight the various developments that informed and shaped the critique of the 1970s and 1980s. Three seem crucial: the rise of a new sensitivity; the emergence of a new anthropological paradigm; and the availability of new conceptual tools.

A new sensitivity: The late 1960s and early 1970s, when most of those active in the *Writing Culture* critique entered graduate school, were marked by a new and intense sensitivity to matters of power and political discrimination. Behind this new sensitivity was a series of events and movements that decisively shaped the political consciousness of the first post-World-War-II generation. It must suffice here to merely list some of these: the worldwide struggles against colonialism, the rise of the civil rights movements, the coming of affirmative action, the anti-war movement, the Chicago riots, new-nation building, minority movements, etc.[2]

A new anthropological program: At a time when American anthropology was largely dominated, on the one hand, by various conceptions of economic and political development and, on the other hand, by a turn toward British structural-functionalism, Geertz's formulation of an interpretative program for anthropology marked an important event.[3] His intervention was a conceptual one—though with far-reaching methodological implications. Conceptually he proposed understanding culture as text. To be more precise, Geertz conceptualized culture as a semiotic web of meaning. This web, he maintained, could be compared to a script that implicitly organizes—makes meaningful—collective conduct, from everyday patterns of life to complex ritual and religious practices. Methodologically Geertz presented, in accordance with its concept of culture, a philological mode of analysis. What philologists do with ancient cultures, namely read and interpret old text fragments to identify patterns of meaning peculiar to a culture, the anthropologist should do with the cultures she studies.

The challenge of fieldwork was, as he famously remarked, to look over the shoulder of an informant and to read the script that guides the native's life. Gradually, one would assemble notes that shed light on the structure of the text/culture, notes which one could then present, in the form of thick descriptions (another textual practice), in such a way that they show how this text/culture organizes collective conduct and makes it meaningful.[4] For *Writing Culture*—or for those who were to contribute to the critique of the 1980s—Geertz's textual (philological) reconceptualization of fieldwork and ethnography was of wide-ranging significance and influence. First, as a result of the philological turn ethnographies were increasingly understood—or came into view—as texts and thus as literary documents. Second, it was Geertz's program in which most of the participants in *Writing Culture* had been trained and to which they subscribed. It seems justified to say that one central aim of *Writing Culture* was to improve, analytically and politically, the quality of ethnographies as texts.

New conceptual tools: The 1970s, in the United States and beyond, were characterized by the emergence of new conceptual frameworks and modes of thought that were inseparable from the new political awareness and the sensitivity to matters of power and political discrimination. Most of the influential writing came from Europe, particularly from France. Important authors included Louis Althusser, Roland Barthes, Gilles Deleuze, Michel de Certeau, Jacques Derrida, and especially Michel Foucault, who made visible the conjuncture of politics and knowledge.[5] In the United States these authors were first read and discussed in literature departments and hence had their initial influence on literary theory and criticism. For *Writing Culture* they provided the impetus for politicizing the textual understanding of ethnographies Geertz had, if indirectly, brought about. They were precisely the counterpart of the literature to which Geertz opened up the discipline.

If one locates *Writing Culture* at the intersection of these three developments, its distinct form and nature become comprehensible. *Writing Culture* is a political and epistemological critique of "ethnographies as texts." This critique found its distinctive form of expression in a political and intellectual scrutiny of rhetorical conventions. To summarize the key argument of the volume, genre constraints govern the composition of ethnographies. These constraints (or conventions) affirm, if only implicitly, colonial perspectives and asymmetries of power in so far as they lead ethnographers to construct timeless others who have presumptively lived in the same way for hundreds, perhaps thousands, of years; to construct spatially bound cultures and thus deny mobility; and to speak for the other, thus denying the natives a voice of their own. The subtitle, "on the poetics and politics of ethnography," subtly captures this dual focus on rhetoric and power.

The constellation wrought by *Writing Culture* was what James Faubion in our dialogues calls a deparochialization of anthropology—at least for those who participated in it. The volume introduced an irreversible fracture between (a part of) the older generation, which defended the classical project, and (a part of) the younger one, which found itself compelled to move beyond what appeared to them as a repertoire of well-tried concepts, to find new ways of practicing ethnography, new ways of producing anthropological knowledge about the world we inhabit—without parochial guidance. Of course, neither in its dissatisfaction with the traditional ethnographic project nor in its effort to critically reconfigure the practice of anthropology was *Writing Culture* an isolated phenomenon. There were several other critical—in their tendency equally deparochializing—projects underway. One thinks, to mention just a few, of the anthropology of identity, the emergent public culture project, or the burgeoning feminist anthropology. Without taking these other projects—and their various predecessors—into account it is impossible to comprehend the changes anthropology has undergone in and since the 1980s.

And yet, what made *Writing Culture* stand apart from its critical counterparts—or so it seemed to me in the mid-1990s—was that it directed its critique neither to this or that particular aspect of the ethnographic project but to the project as such: It radically put in question all kinds of great divides that had hitherto been, if implicitly, constitutive of ethnography. In so doing, it inaugurated—together with other critical reconfigurations of the discipline—the beginning of another kind of anthropology, the aim of which was to reformulate and restate the anthropological project, to invent new ways of being an anthropologist or ethnographer. How to do so, however, was not evident and thus constituted a challenge that has been greeted as an "experimental moment."[6] It was precisely this experimental moment—its openness—that aroused my curiosity in the mid-1990s.

The chance to discuss some of the paths along which anthropology has developed since the 1980s came to me half a decade after I left Tübingen, namely in form of an exchange of thoughts between Paul Rabinow and George Marcus. In 2002 I was a graduate student at Berkeley who had just started field research in a neurobiology lab in Paris. Rabinow (then my faculty advisor) sent me a draft essay Marcus had sent him in reaction to his soon-to-be-published book *Anthropos Today: Reflections on Modern Equipment* (2003). Part of the intention of *Anthropos Today* was to provide a set of tools for studying conceptual shifts in contemporary forms of reason. What motivated the project was that Rabinow, in his own work on emergent phenomena in the biosciences, had frequently encountered questions and problems for which the classical anthropological repertoire, ranging from culture to fieldwork, was not adequate: "My work does not focus on culture in any of the current senses of the term (meaningful totalities, ordered semiotic fields, multiplying habitus, contested identities, etc.). My research, furthermore, has not taken place in the kind of rural setting in which one expects to find those doing fieldwork. . . . Therefore neither where nor how I conduct my investigations is captured by the term fieldwork. . . . We require a new figuration more appropriate to the changing practice."[7]

In *Anthropos Today* Rabinow sought to respond by presenting the conceptual equipment that has proven productive in his empirical studies of modern forms of reason, namely a "nominalistic" focus on "the contemporary" and on the "assemblages," "apparatuses," and "problematizations" that are constitutive of it.

In the comment he sent to Rabinow, Marcus questioned precisely this call for a "new" figuration of anthropological research: "Rabinow provocatively provides one paradigm for an alternative practice of anthropological research that does away with the primacy given to sacred concepts like fieldwork, ethnography, culture, and the native point of view." Marcus emphasized that he was not unsympathetic, but that he thought Rabinow was going, perhaps, too far: "There is an important debate yet to be had among those who see the need for an explicit creation of an alternative paradigm of research practice in anthropology, especially in the emergence of an 'anthropology of the contemporary.' Some might see more potential for revision of the classic tropes of ethnographic research rather than their necessary replacement. There is much in Rabinow's formulation of an alternative that speaks to the way classic ethnography is constructed."

Marcus articulated his concerns with a particular problem in mind, namely the disciplinary dilemmas and methodological predicaments created by what he calls anthropology's post-1980 turn toward studying "timely events unfolding in the West or elsewhere." Specifically, he has been concerned by the "dramatic" effects this shift is having on "the temporality holding the deeply embedded conception of ethnographic research in place." According to Marcus, a key diacritic of ethnography as method—in Malinowski's canonical schematic, long-term fieldwork carried out through participant observation and centered in a single site—was a temporality of slowness. Its norm was one of patience and gradual, accumulative achievement. And it was according to this norm of slowness and gradual achievement that anthropologists have judged each other and contributed to a common project—knowledge of people and places around the world. "Control of another language, the effect of demonstrating depth of knowledge of another culture, the writing of ethnographies as if the author is telling less than he or she could—in short, all of the perfomative elements of demonstrating ethnographic authority—have depended on the valorization of a temporality of slowness." By turning toward the study of the "here and now"—rather than of the "far-away" and "timeless"—anthropologists experience profound temporal turbulences precisely because they can no longer make assumptions about what is necessary for their method to produce rich ethnographic data—a temporally stable scene and subject of study. The turn to the timely, one could gloss Marcus, captures anthropology much more than anthropology is capable of capturing the timely. The remedy he envisions is to critically revise the anthropological culture of method, grounded in fieldwork, in such a way that it is capable of bridging the gap that separates new fields of research and the available methodological repertoire. The problem, though, is how? How practically to carry out such a revision? How to introduce a new kind of intellectual curiosity into contemporary anthropology? How to give it shape as an ambitious analytical project—or several such projects? According to what ideas would one have to rethink ethnographic practice, in research as well as in writing? And how to do so without being dogmatic?

In more specific terms: What is anthropology today? What could it be? What is distinctly anthropological when the discipline is no longer primarily the ethnographic study of the faraway, cultural Other? What defines objects or subjects as anthropological when what the anthropologist studies is no longer exclusively society or culture? What concepts and logical forms do anthropologists have available as they consider what they are doing? How might we conceive of anthropology as a cogent discipline under revised circumstances, characterized by new themes and new topical arenas, by a focus on contemporary events and problems? What connections between past and present work in anthropology can be established? How might anthropologists make explicit and then transform the tacit expectations of the Malinowskian culture of methodology that still dominates the discipline?

Struggling with these questions, Marcus turns an interested and critical eye to Rabinow's work—specifically to *Anthropos Today* and to what he identifies as the trilogy that preceded it in an "anthropology of the contemporary": *Making PCR* (1996), *French DNA* (1999), and *A Machine to Make a Future* (2004).[8]

When I read the notes Marcus sent to Rabinow, I had the idea of bringing them together in a discussion about some of the directions anthropology took after 1986. What made the prospect of such a conversation compelling, or so it seemed to me, was its promise to capture (some of) the transformations, if this is the right term, anthropology has undergone since the 1980s—to overstate it a bit, the collapse of the conventional division of labor that had assigned to anthropology the terrain of the primitive, the traditional, and the premodern and to the other social sciences the terrain of the modern. It was further compelling because both Marcus and Rabinow had been protagonists in the critique of the 1980s captured in *Writing Culture,* and both, in their own particular ways, have sought since to give shape to the motion that this critique initiated. Rabinow has done so by developing what he has called an "anthropology of reason," or, in its current form, an "anthropology of the contemporary."[9] Marcus has done so as an anthropologist who has taken an ethnographic interest in anthropology itself and who has continuously pursued the mapping of the small lines of the mutation of self-understanding of ethnography.[10]

The prospect of bringing them together, of discussing the ways anthropology has developed since the 1980s, and of debating what they thought is at stake in contemporary anthropology excited me. I asked and both agreed. In April 2004 we met at Rice University and had a series of conversations. James Faubion—professor of anthropology at Rice and colleague of Marcus since 1993, student and friend of Rabinow's since 1983—joined us in several of these discussions. Hence, the book's form—two and sometimes three senior professors in exchange with a (former) graduate student—and its content—what is anthropology today?

When we met at Rice, the dialogue between Rabinow and Marcus soon revolved around contemporary anthropology—on what it is or ought to be. Their respective motives for focusing on "anthropology today" can be seen in the different, but complimentary, ways they take up and address the present.

For Rabinow, "today"—understood as an intellectual category—is a logical and conceptual challenge. The present is a historical, open moment in which what is or has been is, at least potentially, changing. His aim as an "anthropologist of the contemporary" (see Dialogue IV) is to identify, trace, and name such changes. However, to confront new problems that one cannot yet even name, the anthropologist needs to find new concepts suited to the particular phenomena whose significance he or she wishes to explore. Thus, anthropology as it is currently practiced is problematic for Rabinow insofar as it refuses, implicitly or explicitly, to abandon the analytical models that dominated social and cultural thought in the past. Anthropology—so one might gloss his position—cannot enter new terrain while it holds on to concepts and methods no longer suited for understanding contemporary problems.

Marcus's problematizing of the present is different. It is not that he is not interested in Rabinow's questions. He is, but the present occupies him for different reasons. The problem he seeks to name is a disciplinary one. To him, the present is a challenge in terms of disciplinary community, integration, standards, norms and forms, and quality. He wants anthropology as a discipline to thrive, but today it does so in his view only partially, in different and unrelated arenas and camps. He is contemplating the state of the discipline and how, according to what principles, it could be reordered. His answer—and here Rabinow agrees—is pedagogy.[11]

Rabinow and Marcus share a deep care for pedagogy and a sense that to reinvigorate anthropology—as a discipline and as a practice—one needs a pedagogy suited to the challenges anthropologists face today. The problem, though, is—or so they argue—that a pedagogy adequate to the present does not yet exist. It needs to be invented, and this is where their two different approaches become complementary.

Marcus is interested in Rabinow's anthropology of the contemporary as a candidate for a new vision of what anthropology today could be, as a means to reinvigorate it as an analytically and conceptually rigorous practice. To be such a means, however, it needs to be didactically connected to previous anthropological projects. In the dialogues, therefore, he frequently challenges Rabinow with educational concerns. Where Rabinow articulates the analytical aims of his work, where he stresses the need to move onward, Marcus asks him how such aims and how such a move could be taught to students, or, for that matter, to fellow anthropologists who feel uneasy about the new anthropology. Marcus emphasizes that he understands Rabinow's logico-conceptual concerns, but urges him not to do away with such concepts as ethnography or fieldwork or culture because to keep such concepts is an important means of bridging the past and the present and—even more important—the different camps at work today. And Rabinow, confronted with Marcus's search for continuity of anthropology's core concepts, asks him to be conceptually more self-reflective, to identify the implicit nostalgia that informs his care for concepts like culture, participant observation, ethnography, fieldwork, etc. He emphasizes that he understands Marcus, but that to hold on to some of the integral classical concepts, the discipline's internal structure needs to be reformed considerably.

One can see the pattern. Where Rabinow endeavors to move onward and to explore the new, Marcus asks for bridges and connections and wonders how Rabinow's project can be integrated into anthropology. On this level the two meet, challenging and following each other, thereby gradually exploring—and inventing—a common space. The conversations gradually come to consider the virtues and possibilities of the design studio, in which possible aims, concepts, and methods for the anthropology of the contemporary are developed, tested, doubted, improved, and left in their unfinished state for others to take on. Hence the title of our project: *Designs for an Anthropology of the Contemporary*.

Designs for an Anthropology of the Contemporary offers critical but engaged explorations of the openness and the motion characteristic of contemporary anthropology. In a dialogic fashion we think through the current condition of anthropology from various points of view. We trace the events that set anthropology in motion; follow the lines of development that have shaped the discipline since the 1980s; explore the conceptual and methodological challenges of the field as it stands today; and explore the possibilities of building bridges from past to present—bridges, that is to say, that allow us to connect the traditional ethnographic project with the structurally and topically new anthropology on the horizon today. These varied efforts to work through the present condition of anthropology share the aim of developing a set of conceptual tools—designs, we call

DIALOGUE I ANTHROPOLOGY IN MOTION

TR: I would like to begin our conversations by framing what both of you have described as a distinct challenge facing anthropology today. Since the 1980s, anthropologists have moved into new terrains—technoscience, finance, media, law, etc.—but the concepts available to analyze these new terrains are largely survivals of the past, survivals from a time when anthropologists studied the culture and social organization of far-away others. The inevitable result is a profound mismatch between old concepts and new analytical requirements. Said in another, perhaps too schematic way, anthropologists are increasingly studying *timely* phenomena with tools developed to study *people out of time*. On the one hand, this mismatch is exciting for it invites conceptual innovation and demonstrations of analytical skill. On the other hand, it is unsettling, for the necessary innovation implies a thorough revision of the concepts, problems, questions, and topics that have been constitutive of the discipline. Ultimately, the challenge is to restate anthropology in relation to its classical tropes. Both of you agree with this broad task but there are some differences in the ways you would pursue it. Before we explore these differences, let's talk about how contemporary anthropology has been set in motion. Why did anthropologists enter into new research arenas? A good point of departure for discussing this question might be the critique of the 1980s that was epitomized in *Writing Culture*, an intellectual movement in which both of you have been protagonists. What happened? What were your dissatisfactions with anthropology as it existed in the United States in the 1960s and 1970s?

PR: In America, at least, the shift you note began well before the 1980s. And there is a specific prehistory to *Writing Culture*, centered on the figure of Clifford Geertz[1] and the joint Harvard, MIT, and Ford Foundation projects of the 1950s that had combined Max Weber, Talcott Parsons, and the ambitious projects of the Harvard Social Relations group.[2] The ideas of a carefully conceived and conceptually worked-out multidisciplinary project of research were put into practice on a large scale in Indonesia. Thus, Geertz was initially a forerunner in rethinking and reorienting the practices of the social sciences in general and anthropology in particular. So maybe that period would be a place to begin.

GM: There certainly was a more authoritative model of how one became an anthropologist in the days of the Harvard and MIT projects[3] to which you refer. Of course, however much is owed to the pre-World-War-II era when Malinowski and Boas pioneered the discipline's distinctive research practices,[4] that model was undergoing change. This was especially true in the United States during anthropology's short post-war expansion, the twilight of its Golden Age,[5] which coincided with Cold War investments in academic expertise, notably area studies, with "development" being the common problem, and ending by the time Paul and I were becoming professors. Actually, we were its beneficiaries as students in elite graduate programs.

TR: Was there continuity between Boasian and post-war anthropology in the sense that anthropology remained concerned with the faraway other, located in "our" past?

GM: Yes. And in retrospect, what is most remarkable and striking in my view is the rupture that the period of the 1980s through the early 1990s marked and produced in the specific kinds of questions, topics, and quite deep traditions of inquiry with which anthropology had been concerned and through which it defined itself. The *Writing Culture* critiques and the debates they stimulated were only the catalyst, however powerful. Geertz is an interesting, towering, transitional figure in terms of the rupture that took place. I think he was the first figure who, even though still of the Golden Age and deeply within anthropology's traditional concerns, under the guise of symbolic anthropology, and then interpretive anthropology, also practiced an anthropology that centrally engaged other disciplines. I'm thinking here of his distinctive contributions to the modernization/ development paradigm of the day—the Harvard-MIT development projects in Indonesia and later the New Nations Committee at Chicago[6]—to the flowering of his interest in the theories and philosophies that informed the study of literature and the humanities generally. That's how I see his enduring importance; he legitimated the stature and presence of anthropology in the interdisciplinary domains and peripheries where it now thrives (and not necessarily in ways he would have endorsed). He forged a presence and constituency for anthropology, by dint of a personal style of writing rather than forming a "school." He legitimated a different kind of core anthropology without it really ever being a project.

PR: I think that distinction is very important. Talcott Parsons at Harvard basically assigned "culture" to a small group of people, the most prominent of whom were Clifford Geertz and Robert Bellah.[7] Bellah took up the Weberian project in Japan, asking, how did it become industrial and modern in the light of its cultural singularity? And Geertz's role was to develop and advance a theory of culture set within a neo-Weberian project of development at a time of decolonization. A version of this project was continued at the University of Chicago in the Committee on New Nations. However, the Vietnam War and the crisis of the development model brought all that to an end for Geertz. Others like Bernard Cohn[8] continued in a more critical mode, for example, engaging actively with subaltern studies.

TR: So, Geertz's focus on culture goes back to Harvard and Talcott Parsons?

PR: It was part of the Harvard project to construct a total human science that would be multi-disciplinary, divided into specific analytical areas, graphically ordered in Parsons's famous tables, and unified under a "general theory of action."[9] The project did not endure whether conceptually, institutionally, or politically. Thus, George's point that anthropologists were marginal is true, though for awhile at least, even after his "interpretive turn" in the early 1970s, Geertz was touted as a great trailblazer of a new social science. For example, he was the first social scientist to be appointed at the Institute for Advanced Study in Princeton.[10] Unfortunately, his tenure there turned into a failed opportunity to build something substantial and enduring.

GM: What distinguishes the present from Geertz's heyday is that anthropology then had a slot to participate in, a secure but marginal slot at what I would call its interdisciplinary peripheries. It was largely a social science slot in a neocolonial project of development. Today, anthropology's engagements have shifted. They are less with social sciences and more with what remains institutionally of the humanities-focused movements of the 1980s and 1990s, of which *Writing Culture* was a part and expression. In recent years anthropology's research agendas have been defined by the terms and frameworks produced by those conversations, perhaps because they brought to culture and difference, which have historically been formative of anthropology itself, new theoretical and conceptual resources. Anthropology has transformed itself internally through this shift in the direction of its most important interdisciplinary alliances. Yet, I find it curious that anthropology's interdisciplinary partners, for example in literary and cultural studies, seem to be oblivious to the changes they have wrought in this field. What they know of anthropology is what the *Writing Culture* critique indeed revised and updated, rather than what happened after *Writing Culture*. Often, when I meet someone from a literature department today, or anyone of the general public for that matter, they still think what anthropologists have to say comes out of the experience of studying peoples like the Trobriand Islanders,[11] in relative isolation, even though the discourse and research concerns of anthropology are now much more expansive and diffuse. I suppose, in some sense, that the humanities (and a mainstream public) need anthropology to keep representing the "primitive."

TR: And this "expansive and diffuse discourse" is what we want to address as a symptom of the contemporary condition of anthropology?

GM: What most interests me in this symptom is what could recreate a density of *technical consideration* amid all this diversity of work within the discipline and even if that can be done at all now. What counts as data in research—as ethnography? Is ethnography mainly about data anymore? What forms do data take, and how distinctive are they? And if anthropological knowledge is not significantly based on technical considerations, as in the past history of ethnography, then what? If the writ for ethnography is still descriptive analysis, but if ethnographies today are more complex documents of research experiences that the training models and process do not sufficiently imagine, or only thinly control, then what?

DISSATISFACTIONS AND PERSONAL TRAJECTORIES

TR: You both seem to agree that anthropology, in the 1960s and 70s, had a secure project and position, and yet, both of you were dissatisfied with the state of the anthropological project as it was. Why? What was wrong with the Harvard project of a total human science?

JF: George, you yourself arrived at Harvard's Department of Social Relations to witness its crumbling. That was clearly crucial to your own sensibility with respect to anthropology.

PR: What year?

GM: I was supposed to go to graduate school at Harvard in 1968 but I deferred it for a fellowship at Cambridge University and then was drafted into the Army. I came back to Harvard in 1971. I entered Social Relations with an emphasis in anthropology but ended up with a Ph.D. from the anthropology department. Within four years of my arrival, Social Relations had disappeared. It felt like the end of a historic project in interdisciplinary optimism. Talcott Parsons was still there, giving abstract lectures reminiscent of some heyday, but mostly to foreign students . . .

PR: . . . such as Niklas Luhmann.[12]

GM: Social anthropology at Harvard in the early 1970s had retreated into its most traditional forms. But what impressed me most was an intellectual underground or invisible college, especially among theory-oriented students who had been in Social Relations. For instance, none of the French writers who would become important to thinking about culture, such as Foucault, Lacan, Derrida, et al. were read in the courses I took at Harvard in anthropology, social relations, or elsewhere. Marxist theory was big at the time—Althusser, Godelier, the early Habermas. The poststructuralist thinkers were what students were talking about, reading these works on their own. So I belong to a generation in which we were trained traditionally but with this background reading of works in translation in the early 1970s. And this is where our energy and excitement were found.

PR: In Chicago, things were not crumbling in those years, quite the opposite (even though Geertz left in 1970). I was there during the 1960s (B.A., M.A., Ph.D.), and we were reading French and German work in the core courses, and that continued in different ways when Victor Turner[13] and Marshall Sahlins[14] came, and even more so with the Comaroffs.[15] I have not had the same sense of rupture and rebellion against the discipline because I was always oriented to a broader conception of the "cultural sciences" of the Weberian kind. Hence I have less disappointment in the existing discipline than you do, although I share many of your dissatisfactions with existing anthropology. This broader view of anthropology in a classic theoretical tradition is what one might call the "Chicago effect," and which one sees in so many Chicago students of my generation and up to the present. I saw anthropology as one discipline among others in the interpretive social sciences, understood with a good deal of historical depth and comparative reach.

TR: Though in *Reflections on Fieldwork in Morocco*[16] you say, a bit like George, that there was a clear gap between students and the faculty. You write that Thomas Kuhn's term "paradigm exhaustion" captured the atmosphere you found yourself in.[17] So what was exhausted?

PR: Most significantly it was the politics, because this was during the Vietnam War and Geertz was basically in favor of the Vietnam War, albeit in a nuanced and doubt-ridden manner. And then there was a more existential sense, which we might have complex reversals on here, that the American academy was moving toward ever more specialization under pressure from the Cold War apparatus; the Hutchins model[18] of a comprehensive curriculum and *Bildung* appeared to be in trouble even at Chicago. Fortunately, to a surprising extent, that model of pedagogy has endured. I went into anthropology in many ways for existential reasons both personal and political. These broader crises fed a sense of alienation, but the problem wasn't that we weren't allowed to read Gadamer or Ricœur. I mean, Geertz was writing about Ricœur.[19] I first heard about Foucault as an undergraduate in a reading course on Buddhism that I was doing with the historian of religions, Mircea Eliade, who thought Foucault's view of history was too static. So Harvard and Chicago were different in this respect.

JF: But didn't your disillusionment, the one that Tobias articulated with regard to *Reflections on Fieldwork*, have to do with Hutchins's idea of the university? Isn't that what you and your generation had come to see, largely for political reasons, as altogether too imperialistic and ethnocentric?

PR: Not entirely. I thought there was complicity, betrayal, and alienation, but not because the intellectual life at Chicago was impoverished or irrelevant. Sitting there and listening to Hannah Arendt, Hans Morgenthau, Leo Strauss, Raymond Aron, Louis Dumont, or Claude Lévi-Strauss, and Richard McKeon, I was not alienated from thinking, and I'm still not alienated from it. Of course, this does not mean that I agreed with everything I heard. Consensus was hardly the ethos at Chicago; argument was cherished. The Strauss circle never tempted me, although it was fascinating for a young American to hear this diminutive man talking with such passion and authority about Spinoza or Plato. On the philosophic side, the main influence for me was Richard McKeon. He was an Aristotelian and a pragmatist. McKeon was fundamentally opposed to Strauss and others who privileged the past over a supposedly fallen modernity. McKeon thought that was a dangerous and false opposition.

Chicago had a deep seriousness and provided a sustained intellectual training that the American university in general needs to reaffirm. There was awareness that the University of Chicago as an institution was complicit with the racism implicit in and abetted by urban renewal, and that the core curriculum was not consistently energetic enough in making connections to the larger geopolitics of America and the world. That being said, one should remember that David Schneider[20] and Barney Cohn, among others, were making those connections with clarity and passion. It is worth remembering that anthropologists as different as Arjun Appadurai,[21] Nick Dirks,[22] and I are all deeply indebted to Barney Cohn.

JF: This is worth continuing to articulate. This is what George has called the Chicago high-mindedness.

PR: But high-mindedness, via Cohn and Schneider or Arendt, was never separated from power relations and institutional critique. The dissatisfactions were complex. I just felt then and I feel today that there's nothing fundamentally wrong with that model of pedagogy and inquiry except that it's been betrayed by its more recent ideologues and acolytes like Allan Bloom.[23] Bloom's attacks on "theory," his resistance to new social movements and the like were all counter-modern in their ethos and eventuated in the neo-conservative movement. This development showed me how contingent the relationship between thinking and practice can be. McKeon worked on the U.N. Charter, saw no impediment to enriching philosophy by making it multi-civilizational, always taught that thinking of any importance arose out of problematic situations (from Aristotle to Dewey). There was no intrinsic reason whatsoever that critical and pragmatic thought could not flourish in modernity and beyond. I was taught to believe that there was a type of legitimacy to the modern age that took the form of both a problem and a task. There was no "before" and "after" thought. McKeon would cite both Ockham and Heidegger and show they illuminated current issues while in other ways being simply discordant from each other and from the present.

GM: I didn't identify with Harvard or its tradition that much. I repeatedly entered places for study and training where whatever was visionary or promising in anthropology had peaked (for example, social anthropology at Cambridge in 1969; ethnoscience at Yale in the late 1960s; social relations at Harvard in the early 1970s). I mean, from the outset, what I found inspiring in anthropology was the experience of fieldwork. So my student history of engagement with anthropology has always been peculiar. There was always this gap for me in my excitement about the field and the less exciting ways it was being practiced in those famous places that I passed through for training. Rather than a lineage of academic descent that I could claim had formed me, I passed through the sacred sites, but obliquely, so to speak. So I have always felt that I was never well trained in anthropology in any of its Golden-Age forms, and this has had certain advantages even, in retrospect. This cleaving to and away from anthropology was true of most of the Harvard students in my period there—I recall that my fellow students at Harvard were always going off to lectures elsewhere—to Stanley Cavell, Barrington Moore, Daniel Bell, and several others. What kept me centered and going in anthropology was the focus of training in the doing of fieldwork. Associated with a project on conflict management in Pacific societies, I did quite traditional fieldwork in the Kingdom of Tonga, according to the training ethos that was then in effect and is still in effect.[24] But I had not internalized with any specificity any of the reigning models at that time that taught one to give a conceptual frame and gloss to what one was doing. So I came back, and I did the dissertation rather idiosyncratically within the norm of writing from fieldwork. Not grandly, but idiosyncratically.

TOWARD WRITING CULTURE

TR: When did you go to Rice?

GM: In 1975. One of the first courses I taught at Rice was "Classics in Ethnography." Dick Cushman (now deceased) and I began to examine the tropes of ethnography.[25] Soon I came across Jim Clifford's publications on Maurice Leenhardt.[26] I had known Jim slightly at Harvard, where he had been in the history department but also participated at the edges of the anthropology department. He came to parties, seminars. He stood out for his impressive questions and discussion at departmental events; he knew something that the rest of us did not know, especially about the French tradition of anthropology, but, I thought, needed to know. When we were rebuilding the Rice anthropology department, and focusing on questions of rhetoric and discourse, I invited Jim for a talk. He brought with him a whole bag of resources—not only early drafts of his now-famous essays but also stacks of French publications by anthropologists that were new to us. It was a catalytic moment. His visit revealed a process of consilience at work in the questions in which we were locally interested. A sense of possibility in critique.

JF: I think it's important that some attention be given to the volume Dell Hymes edited, *Reinventing Anthropology*, and that moment of the critique of the discipline. It's crucial to recognize that it is not the same kind of critique, not nearly so profound a critique of the discipline that emerged later in *Writing Culture*. It's a critique of the politics of the discipline, emerging immediately in the context of the Vietnam War but absolutely faithful to the discipline itself—and absolutely faithful to science and the discipline as science. *Reinventing Anthropology* is an expression of an intention to render the discipline in the service of the right kind of politics.

PR: That's right.

JF: Whereas the *Writing Culture* critique is at a remove from any practical, applied disciplinary outcome and is far more an intellectual critique than a political critique of the discipline.

GM: *Writing Culture* came from a certain kind of appropriation of anthropology—or at least from a momentary special interest in it—within strong new critical trends in the humanities, and that colored very much its impact and reception. The research agendas in anthropology in rhetoric and concept were importantly refashioned by the discussions *Writing Culture* received within intellectual movements then flourishing in the humanities. Together, they justify the term "rupture," as I said. So, anthropology's current predicament is that while its aesthetics and ethos of practice are intact—that is, fieldwork, ethnography—it has intellectually taken on additional genealogies, and is working within discourses not primarily of its own disciplinary making. This has plusses and minuses, but for me mainly minuses, or at least problems, when it tries to do so with the same distinctive aesthetics of practice and method. After all it was precisely fieldwork/ethnography that the humanities did not do and that anthropology persists in doing.

PR: *Reinventing Anthropology* first presaged strands of later postcolonial studies, both in its broad politicized stance as well as the unexamined moralism of much of it. I see a lot of continuity between its concerns and the mainstream of the discipline today. But for me it had little impact on my thinking, partially because I had been much more involved in France. It was not news to me that there had been colonialism, and so I was looking to [Georges] Balandier, [Georges] Condominas, [Michel] Leiris, and Sartre—and Moroccan and Algerian novelists, not to mention Ho Chi Minh—rather than to Gerald Berreman.[27]

During the Vietnam War, the majority of the American Left was for the most part uninterested and uninformed about the Vietnamese. Of course this was less true in France because of its long-term, violent, and much-contested colonial relations and because of the broader scope of the French political scene. So, partly out of protest, I started learning Vietnamese, though the only course in English available then was a U.S. Army course, and by volume two it was teaching people how to call in air strikes—so our little group stopped. The kind of critical intellectual space that anthropology seemed to me to offer demanded that one know something about the language and history of those involved in the war. What anthropologists should have been doing all the way through, and I continue to feel this, was to learn and know the history of Vietnam, its complex relations with China, its rich tradition of resistance, its poetry. The number of American experts and scholars who knew the history of Vietnam even during the war, not to mention who knew the language, was miniscule. Although scholars such as Alexander Woodside[28] and David Marr[29] were inspirational.

I became an anthropologist in many ways because I felt, and continue to feel, profoundly alienated from the United States. And, hence, anthropology for me, no doubt naively, was a place for those alienated from the officially sanctioned discussions. It was for people who cared about what was going on below, beyond, and between acceptable discourse. Critical thinking has the task of operating in the future inter-zones.

GM: There's an existential issue here. Anthropology, I think, encourages these sorts of strong feelings about public issues and the world, be they alienation, idealism, or something else. When I meet any anthropologist, I presume there is such a motivating well of feelings in him or her somewhere, and those feelings are not too far from what he or she does as a researcher and scholar. Anthropology allows for, even expects, this proximity far more so than other disciplines, especially those among the social sciences. But previously the modes of expression for these motivating orientations within the research models had been much too impoverished in the prevailing rhetorics for writing about fieldwork. So there has always been a well and surplus of unarticulated insights and experiences from fieldwork on which movements of innovation and new thinking could be generated in the discipline.

In its own time, I do not think the Dell Hymes's book was as strongly transforming of the discipline as it might have been because there was so much of what defined its purpose and style going on elsewhere, in the turbulence of social discourse, and of writing generally in U.S. intellectual life. *Writing Culture* was a more consequential moment in relation to anthropology or the idea of social science in the United States. It represented a widespread, mostly unarticulated feeling in a very conservative moment, a very blah moment, whereas *Reinventing Anthropology* came out of something that was alive in the society with a broad-based movement of protest fueling it.

But the particular moment in the development of an anthropologist in which I am especially interested is that very moment in which a student feels that there is something lacking or insufficient in the model of research that anthropology offers—the challenge, the romantic remaking of the self, a way of doing good, a source of estrangement good for thought—the very thing that brought him into the discipline in the first place. I think this issue is neglected in the usual accounts of the history of anthropology, and for which confessional tales of apprentice fieldwork are inadequate. For the story that we're telling here, the predicament of students today in becoming professionals is crucial.

PR: Right, and hence *Reflections on Fieldwork in Morocco* was perceived to break with the run of the mill of fieldwork accounts that were already quite developed by the late 1970s[30]—but always delegitimated as not being science—because, I think, it picked up on these themes.

GM: Indeed, *Reflections* was subversive in 1977, marked by the accidental emergence of the project of writing it and then its difficult gestation in coming to publication. But that was absolutely crucial to its enduring significance. *Writing Culture* had two important effects: to make explicit the inadequacy of standard forms of ethnographic writing in dealing with the realities of fieldwork and, therefore, to encourage a critique of the actual process of research itself, of fieldwork. The former effect occurred, in excess, from the 1980s on; the latter has hardly occurred at all. But the process of research is now very much in question because of the ways the world has changed and how these changes press on the conditions for conceptualizing and doing fieldwork.

PR: *Reflections on Fieldwork* has just marked its thirtieth year in print in a new edition, so apparently there is less dissonance between conceptual work, experimental narrative self-reflection, and accessibility than your perspective would suggest. The structure of the book, after all, was taken from Hegel's *Phenomenology of Spirit*.

DEPAROCHIALIZATION

JF: Would the two of you, given that you were both participants, accept the characterization that the project of *Writing Culture* was an attempt to deparochialize the discipline?

GM: Yes. It did do that but it did it without discipline, project, or coherent thinking about an alternative vision for anthropology. And that's our problem today.

PR: There was a great need for new concepts to fit the new experiences that were going on as well as the new problems that were emerging. *Writing Culture* deparochialized, to use Jim's term, sectors of American anthropology. Deparochialization is part of *Writing Culture*'s reception. It was part of a wave that introduced diverse strains of European thought—I'm thinking here of the Frankfurt School, not deconstruction—into literature faculties and the general culture of the elite American universities. These trends had been hotly debated since the late 1960s in places like Yale and Johns Hopkins, but remained policed by and large out of anthropology. Combined with this void was a refusal on the part of the most respected intellectual voices in the field—Marshall Sahlins, Eric Wolf,[31] or Clifford Geertz, to name a few, people who knew these debates, these concepts—to integrate them and so to broaden the canon. Indeed, they actively sought to keep them out. Think of Sahlins or Geertz on Derrida, or Foucault or Bourdieu,[32] and cringe. *Writing Culture* was a refraction of a massive change that had already happened in the humanities in the United States. Some of us and many students were open to this change that the discipline policed or sought to domesticate. Geertz or Sahlins could have joined this debate in a critical and productive fashion, but they didn't do it. Geertz published *The Interpretation of Cultures* in 1973, and even in 1986, when *Writing Culture* was published, he could have engaged the issues, but he consistently refused, relegating his remarks to contemptuous footnotes. Even today Sahlins writes pamphlets mocking the non-canonical (to him) French.[33] Unwittingly, as it turned out, by their refusal to engage in critical discussion, by their despising the present, they essentially foreclosed their own futures. This was a loss to the discipline.

TR: Yes, Geertz famously critiqued you, Dwyer, and Crapanzano.[34] But what were the reactions of the broader anthropological readership? What about the Left, for example, the people who had participated in *Reinventing Anthropology*?

PR: It was rejected as well by the orthodox Left. *Writing Culture* was a combination of people who considered themselves Leftists of one stripe or another and were certainly conscious of feminism, of gay movements, and social movements more broadly, even if these topics were not explicitly represented in a forceful manner in the initial rendition. It was not as diverse as it should have been. So it was a critical project but it was refused by Laura Nader,[35] Gerald Berreman, Eleanor Leacock,[36] and, for that matter, Sherry Ortner[37] and a lot of other people. *Writing Culture* opened a space, which became quite a fertile space, even if not a dominant force with lasting impact in anthropology.

JF: It's crucial to underscore why it was rejected by the orthodox Left and that is because the orthodox Left cannot—could not and cannot—do without science. It must represent the truth. It must have scientific socialism on its side, right? Most of the stances included in *Writing Culture* were too epistemologically complicated.

PR: It has to have two things: science and a theory of history. *Writing Culture* was nominalistic. It was open. It didn't know where it was going. It pointed to profound inadequacies in all of these other mega- and meta-stories—where the Third World was going, where America was going, where capitalism was going. Of course, we all knew that Althusser or Gramsci existed, but we felt that the level at which they approached things left out the revealing and significant details of the real world. The exemplary example was the "Coke can in the Trobriand picture" that needed to be airbrushed out, as Jim Clifford would say with a wry smile. We knew that the "primitive" was drinking Coke in many parts of the world. Our challenge was to be true to what we knew to be there. My entry into what became *Writing Culture* was through my interaction with Jim Clifford. We had met in Paris, I believe, or in any case because we shared an interest in French thought and had mutual friends there. For several years running we co-taught a seminar in which the Berkeley students once a month would go down to Santa Cruz where they would cook for us, and vice versa. We had a series of distinguished guests including Edward Said, Hayden White, and David Schneider. I had an agonistic relationship to what I took to be Jim's much more literary style of thought, though I was convinced that much of his work was first-rate, especially his book on Maurice Leenhardt. I think at times he took the agonism for antagonism. I entered into the conference in Santa Fe[38] positioned as marginal and remained so afterward, though, again, in the very broad scope of things I felt there was much of value that was being articulated.

TR: When we talk about deparochialization, Marxism, and the intellectual Left, what was the place of Eric Wolf and his students in relation to *Writing Culture*?

PR: Utter and complete rejection. Eric Wolf, Marvin Harris,[39] and their partners and allies chased an entire cohort of the University of Chicago students out of New York. We had a group that met at Sherry Ortner and Bobby Paul's[40] apartment. There were fifteen or twenty of us in New York, and not all from Chicago but Chicago-style. We were sort of the left Geertzians or the left Schneiderians. But we were ostracized. For example, I was never allowed to teach a graduate course at CUNY. They marginalized us because they despised Geertz and Lévi-Strauss and they just saw this as some kind of, I don't know what, right-wing thinking of some sort or other. Who knows? In my eyes, it was an exercise of raw power. When I asked Geertz to intervene, he said something to the effect, "People I know have never heard of Marvin Harris." Raw power meets unabashed elitism—educational but despairing.

GM: It's interesting because this kind of internal history of anthropology never had as strong an impact on me because . . .

PR: You had a good job!

GM: Well, I was not victimized by this kind of interesting, painful politics of faction and purge. I had heard of this story about the Chicago types that were kicked out of New York, but while it has a lot to do with your biography, it seems to have little to do with what preoccupies you now. Intellectually, so little is left of those controversies and feuds. Today there is *no* anthropological canon that influences how students think about and find terms for what they're doing as research. What is most influential is the retailing of a vast range of more recent works across disciplines. Intellectually, there is this kind of complex political history that has pushed you and your generation in one direction or another but you have continued to grow and develop in ways that those old controversies could never have conceived. But the typical professor of our generation is now left with the question, what do I have students read of the anthropological canon as they are increasingly oriented to moves they can use in very recent work shaped by interdisciplinary tastes?

PR: I completely agree.

GM: So my point is that what's interesting in retrospect is how profoundly it all fell apart.

JF: I would definitely underscore that. That's also, though, why I think that the Hymes volume actually started the process of the undermining of a canon in the discipline. It did so above all in its rejection of the structure-functionalist tradition in its near entirety as inherently politically conservative and so scientifically unacceptable. It was logically overreaching, to be sure, but consequential. Bob Scholte's essay,[41] in particular, also inaugurates the call for a "reflexive and critical" anthropology, even if the terms of both reflection and critique remain distinctly Marxist. It's worth noting that Scholte is indebted in that essay to the early Johannes Fabian,[42] and that the debt signals what might be called the "retemporalization" of the anthropological subject (and the anthropological text). That project continued with a flurry of now canonical critiques of the denial of the historical consciousness and historical coevalness of the primitive, from Richard Price's *First-Time*[43] and Renato Rosaldo's *Ilongot Headhunting*[44] to Eric Wolf's *Europe and the People without History* to Fabian's own *Time and the Other*.[45] So *Writing Culture* by no means arises altogether without precedent, much less ex nihilo. But it carries its precedents much further, reflexively and critically, than the precedents had themselves ventured. It put the anthropological past in all its expressions effectively in suspension—and by no means for political reasons alone.

TR: Also, I think it must be said that in its deparochializing effort *Writing Culture* was hardly alone, right?

JF: Absolutely. For example, it was arguably close to the anthropology of identity that flourished at the time, a project that certainly had deparochializing ambitions of its own. But while *Writing Culture* was close to the interest in identity, it also stood clearly apart from it. As a political critique, its emphasis lies far more in the questioning and exposure of domination and exclusion than in practical advocacy of the oppressed or the championing of specific strategies of their empowerment. It is more centrally an intellectual critique, and there its emphasis lies in questioning both the scientific pretensions and the cognitive conservatism of a discipline relying on a repertoire of well-tried concepts at the expense of considering, acquiring, or inventing new concepts better suited to coming to terms with and to illuminating a thoroughly and ubiquitously modern world.

Another significant deparochializing project to which *Writing Culture* was close and yet far was the feminist anthropology emerging at the time. Perhaps one could capture the difference by saying that of the divide between theoretical generalism and interpretive particularism the contributors to *Writing Culture* have been on the interpretive and particularist side, while, with the notable exception of Marilyn Strathern, most of the feminist anthropologists of the period—Michelle Rosaldo, Louise Lamphere, Sherry Ortner, Sylvia Yanagisako, Jane Collier, Rayna Rapp, and others—were squarely on the other side, committed to generalist programs of analysis however diverse their particular approaches and projects have otherwise been.[46] *Writing Culture* is not a feminist tract. Nor, however, does it deny that the feminists, too, were at work on disciplinary deparochialization, and to good effect.

Finally one may mention—as several critiques have—that in its broad dissatisfaction with anthropology past, *Writing Culture* was not without disciplinary precedents. This critique is partly justified and perhaps there has been a failure to give credit where credit is due. But that being said, it seems justified to say that the volume carries out a critique of the discipline more radical than any of its precursors or of its deparochializing counterparts—namely an epistemological critique that puts its very project in question.

LONG LIVE ANTHROPOLOGY

G M : *Writing Culture* was viewed in largely negative terms in anthropology. It did the job of opening up or of demolition, depending on how you look at it, without putting anything else in place. As I think of *Writing Culture* now, it maintained the mise-en-scène of traditional anthropology in a refurbished form. Even though it addressed critically the problem of the Malinowskian encounter with the Other, it was still framed by that problem even if its moment had passed. Afterward there were years of variations on *Reflections on Fieldwork in Morocco* and on the kind of ethnography that feminist writers pioneered before and after *Writing Culture*. For a while what was left were certain secondary or residual paradigms that had been established in the 1960s, such as the Marxist anthropology of Eric Wolf and others. They had the opportunity to a fill a certain void or answer a desire for a big paradigm but they failed intellectually to take advantage of the moment. The end of the Soviet Union and hopes for socialism severely undermined Marxist movements such as they were in the U.S. academy, and indeed leadership in the anthropology-history nexus became dominated by postcolonial writers who were intellectually part of the same currents as *Writing Culture.*

PR: Sydel Silverman[47] took over the Wenner-Gren Foundation. Marvin Harris was a surprisingly powerful figure writing textbooks. Eric Wolf was exercising power in a strategic manner and then, as you say, it totally imploded at some point. Part of the retrograde and complex reaction that we're about to get into in the 1990s turns on the fact that the conceptual apparatus was stuck, but the leading figures who retained institutional power were ultimately unscientific in their refusal to change, to modify their thinking, to address new objects.

GM: So, yes, they have power over the beans, in relative terms, but they retained power while the discipline declined, perhaps along with the rest of the "soft" social sciences. And although anthropology becomes strongly re-established in the interdisciplinary movements of the humanities, even this fashion lost a bit of its glow by the end of the 1980s, and the humanities today provide few resources for anthropology . . .

PR: It continues to matter who has power over the beans.

GM: This is the thing about the 1980s. The institution of anthropology, its profile in its traditional haunts, declines. In any case, anthropology has always been on the margins of the social sciences, a supplementary discipline to mainstream projects organized by other disciplines (certainly true of the development paradigm)—that's what it cost to go its own way. How its partners and constituencies within academia, and outside too, have thought about anthropology and its usefulness has been crucial to its fortunes, institutionally. So, for example, when area studies rises, anthropology rises with it. Otherwise anthropology is stuck in the museum. The stereotypic receptions of anthropology have not really changed all that much. I would say that the *Writing Culture* critique only temporarily disturbed them, if it did so at all. Today the literature professor still thinks of anthropology as some sort of supplement to Rousseau in her thinking about difference for which the lineage of the "primitive" is still necessary.

Sometime in the early 1990s, I became very aware of and struck by the self-fashioning of a number of successful younger anthropologists. Their terrain of ambition, discussion, and debate was in feminism, media studies, cultural studies, postcolonial studies, and science and technology studies. They made their institutional and administrative homes in departments of anthropology, but they considered the latter to be backwaters, places lacking intellectual coherence and energy, and at best, fonts of symbolic and sentimental affection. So during the 1980s and after, anthropology produced an elite of younger scholars who were and are most productively functioning as anthropologists in the interdisciplinary arenas and intellectual agendas that fueled them. At present, life in anthropology departments, even in the most important ones, provides only a fractured and indirect perspective on "where the action really is." So it is hard to articulate the history of anthropology after the 1980s in any of the terms with which that history of its ideas, its personalities, and its institutional politics and debates could be understood before, not only in textbooks but also in what shaped actors.

TR: What you say resonates strongly with my experience as a student in Germany in the mid-1990s. We read the history of anthropology up to *Writing Culture* and . . .

GM: . . . and there is nothing afterwards, in terms of ready labels or organizing debates, and that's still true!

PR: I think we may differ here again, George. I think parts of anthropology are very alive right now.

GM: I don't think we differ that much. I think anthropology is alive and well but only in the context of the shifts that I have tried to outline. Anthropology is alive in its post-1980s engagements, but these are very different from in its old haunts, in its still stereotypic receptions, and in an institutional life that is still a beneficiary of what some have called its Golden Age.

DIALOGUE II AFTER *WRITING CULTURE*

REFLEXIVITY

TR: If we agree that by the 1980s the classical paradigms for how to do ethnography were weakened or exhausted, what can we say about what emerged?

PR: Well, first there was reflexivity.

GM: Yes, *Writing Culture* legitimated a strong strain of writing ethnography reflexively. It continues, but I think many feel that there has been far too much of it. As a genre form it stood effectively as a practical response to many of the ethical and moral critiques of anthropological research — about its exclusions, its omissions, its acts of bad faith. Reflexivity is strong medicine, but it becomes a little like secular religion, a feeble palliative in the face of one or another enlightened or agnostic critique of what is naively taken for granted as virtuous practice.

TR: But in addition to this reflective response to ethical and moral critique, what new kind of research venues emerged in the course of the 1980s? What kind of large-scale anthropological projects? What new kind of analytical foci?

A FOCUS ON IDENTITY

GM: I think that in the aftermath of *Writing Culture* there has been a remaking of anthropology's traditional interests in the styles, topics, and concepts of cultural analysis. For example, there was a highly motivated appropriation of, or at least interest in, culture in the anthropological sense by various movements of cultural analysis and politics within these interdisciplinary realms. Identity became the keyword. Today many of those projects that invested in identity politics, and identity as the object of cultural analysis, are trying hard to get beyond this concept.

JF: Definitely. Identity was the dominant concept, and if you just look quantitatively at the monographs published from the later 1980s forward and at their titles and subtitles, you see it: over and over and over again, work on identity. It was a part of the discipline already, except that the approach to identity—ethnicity, for example, being the classic one in anthropology—was radically constructivist from Barth's essay[1] forward. I think a lot of people who were graduate students in the later 1980s came into anthropology with these interests already formulated out of other disciplines besides our own. So what you often actually got was a lot of crypto-essentialist work, or the typically celebratory work on people having identities, and so asserting power via the assertions of the identities they have.

TR: What you're saying sounds as if identity was actually an interdisciplinary research topic to which anthropology, trying to redefine itself, searching for new venues of research could contribute.

JF: I would think so. In the aftermath of a fairly devastating critique, identity was to organize a lot of people's projects as a kind of a sun around which a variety of often quite politically inflected interests could orbit together. Multiple currents of feminism, for instance, were, in fact, quite productive in attaching themselves to the same sort of orbit. It brought in gay and lesbian studies, which seemed to me at least to hold the promise of being the next great force of the undoing of humanist essentialism. Unfortunately, it hasn't accomplished very much in anthropology. It is limited work, and I'm not quite certain why. In a way it is a possible program that did not fully take off and it remains to be seen what will happen with it.

TR: But why did this interest in identity come about? It for sure did not come out of the blue, so by what was it prefigured?

JF: I think the explanation has to do with the history of politics. It has to do with the New Social Movements—e.g., environmentalism, feminism, and anti-nuclear activism—and people finding an academic niche appropriate to their own political interests, and I think there was no niche more appropriate than identity because it is so wide open. Margaret Mead and Ruth Benedict and Gregory Bateson sustained a constant interest in the question of personality formations, ethnicity, peoples, and whatnot. That could find its place in anthropology because there was already so much source material there to be used and attached to, even if it wasn't, in fact, really compatible with a lot of the interests and the commitments concerning identity that were brought to it. Anthropology attracts a lot of people out to champion the downtrodden, and attention to identity fits very well as an academic site of that interest as well. I have no intention of denigrating that, but I think that it just happened to be the politics that fell into the discipline at a time when it was wide open to receive effectively anything. It received identity, the issue to which that politics was attached, because of the particularities of its own past as well as of its own condition internally at that moment.

PR: But it does correspond to some degree with the "collapse"—or whatever word would be better—of cultural wholes.

JF: Well, there are a lot of cultural wholes to be had there. In the anthropology of identity, they get grounded in a self—but a self of a collective sort. We may play very cleverly with the issue of whether there is such a thing as the self as a kind of integral entity spatio-temporally, but effectively, it is the substitute for culture itself and it allows methodologically all of the same interpretative devices to be at play as Geertz could deploy talking about culture itself. So I think it's right to see that the turn to the self—in fact, I think it's now very, very vividly the case—was remarkably conservative, given the kinds of politics to which it was attached. Conservative, intellectually speaking.

TR: Could one summarize by saying that identity became a residue of culture? That a focus on identity and later on the self or the collective self has replaced culture? With the consequence that traditional conceptions of culture resurface in new costumes, carrying on assumptions and implications?

JF: Yes. I think so. Identity is the substitute. It comes in as the replacement, the replacement concept of the whole.

GM: Yes, a lot of traditional anthropology that could no longer study kinship, religion, or ritual in isolated cultural units or an area was conserved after the 1980s in the pursuit of these topics around identity issues. And identity served to define a sort of generic common ground for the strong relations that anthropology forged with history and historical study. It constituted, in my view, both the conservative and the progressive mainstreams during the 1980s and after, so that anthropology could remain much as it had been while also being able to absorb the theories, categories, orientations, and styles that the interdisciplinary movements emanating from the humanities had to offer. Culture became all about, "Who are we?" or, "What can we resist or accommodate in the face of change and still remain who we distinctively are?" Important questions, indeed, and the sort of meta-questions which anthropological ethnography was always about.

PR: Well, there is no denying that anthropology lost a lot of its distinctive architecture and rigor in making these changes in the study of cultures—so that it could remain the same.

THE PUBLIC CULTURE PROJECT

TR: What else? I mean in addition to identity? Were there further significant projects giving shape to anthropology?

PR: The Public Culture project,[2] which was informed by a hope for a new public culture, after socialism and after capitalism.

GM: Yes. And to me the Public Culture project emerged out of a new tendency in work surrounding *Writing Culture*. It involved a theoretically committed, self-consciously cosmopolitan anthropology that cultivated a role as intellectuals operating in the ideal of a global public sphere, which seemed to be coming into being in the 1980s. This was, and is, the Public Culture project, which Paul mentioned before. To me, this initiative was more interesting than the turn to identity or reflexive anthropology because it recognized that the conditions for the production of anthropology had changed demographically, politically, and in terms of its objects of study. The Public Culture project—focused on contemporary ideas of the public sphere and the debates that could be had there—was, from the late 1980s until the late 1990s, very influential.

PR: Does influential mean successful?

GM: I think both, influential and therefore successful in the way *Writing Culture* was for a moment, but not successful in the sense of establishing a self-generating cross-disciplinary project of research. The journal *Public Culture* was a unique and much needed place to explore ideas and styles in the given trends of cultural analysis and politics, which most crucially were not parochial geographically. *Public Culture* provided the ground for rethinking the whole idea of area studies—not definitively, but it did facilitate the reaccommodation of area studies to a kind of *Writing Culture*–influenced anthropology. There was a lot of remaking that was done in the Public Culture group that derived from predominantly Chicago-networked anthropology.[3]

TR: What do you mean by "remaking"?

GM: It offered a place for people who might still go to far-off places and study ordinary people, but who would report something from this research that was not the usual thing in your standard anthropology journals. It enacted a practice for anthropology within the early academic discussions of globalization. Most importantly, it also provided both a transnational readership and participation for this work. So it was made for anthropologists who were studying topics like advertising in Mumbai,[4] which, at that time, were uncommon in the *American Anthropologist* and the *American Ethnologist*.

TR: I think one has to mention here, as well, that later, in the early 1990s, *Public Culture* played an important role in formulating a cultural anthropology of globalization. Arjun Appadurai and others have reformulated the culture concept and made it central for the understanding of the flux of people and things in the age of globalization. The idea was as simple as it was compelling: If a globalized world is a culturally heterogeneous world, in which people and things are in flux, then "cultural" anthropology has a major contribution to make for the understanding and conceptualization of a global cultural sphere or a cultural democracy.

JF: Well, I think one must also note the shift toward the objective. For a good two decades now, there has been an increasing turn toward objects and the objective. Appadurai's *Social Life of Things*,[5] which appeared the same year as *Writing Culture*, is an early benchmark of a shift of attention that has since snowballed and expanded its terrain. Daniel Miller's work[6]—or, even more, his influence—is an indication of how far the trend has unfolded. One cannot escape noticing a rehabilitation of material culture and cultural material as an entirely legitimate focus of analysis. Increasingly objects are taking, if not center stage, at least as much of the stage in anthropology as people. The revitalization of interest in the material dimensions of the cultural but also a distinct and broader turning of attention toward the constitution not of selves or subjects but of things "out there," of which selves might of course constitute a part but of which they are not necessarily the pivot or in any other sense the privileged party.

It's very interesting that when my first book[7] was being peer-reviewed, every single reviewer said that it was ethnographically thin until I got to the people. None of them said that in so many words, but all declared the first hundred pages ethnographically thin. Well, it was all about the built environment. It was about symbolic typology and typonomy. It wasn't ethnographically thin if one was supposed to be capturing the particularity of the place. But there weren't any people at the center of it, and that was the problem. Now, however, objects increasingly are taking, if not center stage, then perhaps at least as much of the stage in anthropology as people and, with that shift, I think that one also sees the leaving behind of epistemological problems or epistemological preoccupations about what anthropology can generate or what fieldwork can generate in the way of knowledge.

TR: You mean a shift away from the questions of encounters and how they give rise to knowledge and thus from the authority issues which have been so central to *Writing Culture*?

JF: Yes. In certain respects, some of these older issues of authority or legitimacy, these were all epistemic and epistemological problems. I'm not saying we're leaving epistemology behind in an always sophisticated or well-considered way. There are many questions to be raised about leaving behind that whole set of epistemological questions in favor of an interest in the objects themselves and how to best conceptualize them. Such work is widespread, not just in anthropology but across the disciplines. It's also remarkable in philosophy—this turn away from epistemology toward ontology.

SCIENCE AND TECHNOLOGY STUDIES

TR: It is definitely true for science and technology studies. I think of Latour's[8] work on things or of Rheinberger's "epistemic things"[9] or Lorraine Daston's volumes on *Biographies of Scientific Objects*[10] and *Things that Talk*. And this brings me to my next question: What about science and technology studies? We have talked about identity and public culture, but what was the place and role of science studies, of medical anthropology?

GM: I see science and technology studies (STS) as being the place of real challenge for people who wanted to opt out of identity-dominated cultural analysis. Although the question of ethics and the ethical became one of the explicit arenas in which the relation of science/technology to society has been engaged, STS was relatively free of the heavy load of moralizing discourse and rhetoric that framed cultural analysis from the 1980s on. STS ultimately winds up in the same terrain as other forms of cultural analysis, but through unanticipated routes and new research challenges. It also finally took anthropology beyond the subaltern subject without neglecting that condition of life or perspective. It involved anthropology in a much more complicated space of research, equal to new perceived complexities in the world of the 1990s and beyond, with less of an anticipated path or frame of inquiry.

TR: But that came temporally after identity and public culture, right?

GM: Yes, it was a certain development out of medical anthropology by feminists who were oriented to a much more open kind of theory than that which brought science studies into anthropology as a "branded" field. As an example, I am thinking of the spate of projects around the study of reproductive technology.[11]

JF: Absolutely. At the level of its actual fieldwork production, feminism survives most powerfully in the discipline through its engagement with objects and rationalities, and by no means the least of them the objects and rationalities that come together in the new reproductive technologies. So, it's still the same ambit of issues — the natural and sociocultural dimensions that influence both the conception and the position of women. Are we redrawing the divide between nature and culture? That's already in Strathern's work by the beginning of the 1990s.[12] So, yes, there really is something happening in the world — culture isn't what it used to be, and nature correlatively isn't, either — to which people haven't actually been attending until recently. The attention hasn't been anthropological alone, but when anthropological it has been at its most substantive. That counts as a real achievement.

TR: And that was also the context of new work on kinship, right?

JF: Yes, the whole revival of the analysis of kinship, which was dead as could be in 1986, has largely occurred in the context of STS and medical anthropology.

TR: So, in summary, we have identified as the major trends of research in anthropology since the 1980s: reflexivity, identity, public culture, science studies. And Jim has indicated that in recent years one can see a shift away from the epistemological concerns so dominant in *Writing Culture* toward an interest in things, objects, and rationalities.

JF: I would simply add that it's important to recognize that such trends aren't free-floating but instead have been the hallmarks of particular disciplinary networks, particular cooperatives, the meetings of like minds.

PR: Yes, and if we're looking for groups that are carrying these ideas, the various identity groups are self-evident. The emergence of self-identified populations of one sort or another (gay, native, of color) in the profession is straightforward. And the problems that the earlier, liberal developmentalists (Geertz and company) ultimately had to face have had to be faced again. Revolution — whether liberal or socialist or sexual this time around — didn't work and then the sort of Public Culture aspect of postcoloniality also didn't work. As Ben Lee has said publicly, the global public sphere that they hoped for didn't turn out to be very much like they had hoped. There has been more savage capitalism and less democratic revolution than anticipated.

TRANSFORMATIONS OF THE STUDENT BODY

TR: When we talk about the changes anthropology has undergone since the late 1980s, we should also talk about the transformation in the curiosity of students entering anthropology grad schools. I know that you, Paul, have found these changes significant for the ways anthropology has developed.

PR: For a number of years now, I have been intrigued by the fact that elite students in the qualitative social sciences and humanities in the United States have become so interested in postcolonialism when they had not previously been particularly interested in colonialism. And my hypothesis—meant to provoke—is that the rise of NGOs (which is one of the major events of the 1990s in terms of globalization) opened jobs for perhaps thousands of Ph.D.s in a circuitous way. Many bright young college students, who had read some Foucault and Derrida, aren't quite ready to go to law school so they find their way into NGOs all over the world. Incidentally, this phenomenon of recruitment into NGOs has been studied in France, and it follows a different pattern. The recruitment pool is from workers of the social and health professions. And now, at least at Berkeley, we're seeing an entry into anthropology graduate school of many people who have been through NGOs and have, in a bigger way, run through the crisis of the Peace Corps that we saw earlier—an existential crisis in which the humanitarianism and the "let's go somewhere exotic and let's test ourselves" turns stale at age twenty-five and people realize they don't want to do this for the rest of their lives and, more important, experience a deep and thoughtful crisis about what it all means. At Berkeley we see a growing number of these humanitarians-turned-graduate students. So, I see this pattern as a recruitment vector for some of these movements like public culture and postcolonial studies in anthropology, which have today seemed to run their course.

I see the three vehicles of globalization as being capitalism, life sciences, and humanitarianism. As I explained in a preliminary manner in *Anthropos*

Today, changing practices and significations of life, labor, and language, in Foucault's terms, define a problem space in transition or reproblematization today. Not enough people have bothered to study capitalism on the ground, as it were. An exception is Caitlin Zaloom,[13] who spent two years in London and in Chicago in the pits of the Stock Exchange actually looking at capitalism as a practice, as a way of life—a sort of combination of Thomas Mann's *Buddenbrooks* and Max Weber's *Protestant Ethic*. And now we're beginning to get a wave of people[14] looking at humanitarianism as a problematic way of life and as something that needs to be understood and studied and reflected upon as much as to be put into practice. But none of these projects of thinking through and studying humanitarianism and capitalism and genomics have the raw ideological appeal that is going to win you revolutionary points among colleagues and undergraduates and the media.

JF: Because all of these constituencies still have faith in humanitarianism, perhaps even in spite of its particular failings.

PR: Yes. But its mass appeal aside, I am certain this is an important direction to pursue. I think this is where the anthropological science lies even if it is not where the immediate academic politics is found today.

TR: So, in the 1990s students entering anthropology were no longer predominantly interested in the cultural Other and the classical themes like ritual, myth, magic, and the romance of far-away places?

PR: Not in my experience. Instead they were guided by political interest and/ or humanitarian ideals and values and by their experience of being part of NGOs. And I can see two ways of integrating them into anthropology. One is public culture and/or postcolonial studies. The other is to teach them tools to analyze what they're interested in, namely humanitarianism and its related discourses—capitalism, or the life sciences, or globalization.

TR: And this is precisely what leads or has led to a shift from the ordinary to experts that characterizes the present, a shift away from the traditional emphasis on studying the embedded and the everyday, with the consequence that the old concepts no longer really work and, at least in part, the traditional anthropological seems to wither away, no?

GM: But such a shift leaves its deep marks. A lot is gone, for better or worse, depending upon who you are. Nonetheless, the largely tacit aspects of professional culture, specifically regarding what it has to do with anthropological research, remain. The weakly articulated but still powerful origins of our methods were deeply invested in those topics. The topics might be gone, but there is a very significant residue.

PR: And these former concerns are often wholly inadequate when they are invoked for use with a new object—for example, when someone tries to apply the considerable literature on ritual to contemporary scientists. We used to be taught, and to teach, an article on the "Nacirema,"[15] a parody of the strange customs of the Americans. Everyone knew it was supposed to be funny, but they didn't seem to realize that it signaled a crisis in the anthropological tool kit in the double sense of a coming re-examination of traditional ethnography and a search for concepts and methods adequate to a globalized world. Examples of using the older concepts on contemporary material that are not parodies, unfortunately sound like they were intended to be.

GM: For mainstream anthropology you still have to work in far-away places among ordinary people. This is what is expected of anthropologists, in the field and even more so in the interdisciplinary arenas in which anthropology takes part. Or you have to mark it as distinctively anthropological by the prominent, but sometimes only partly successful, use of signifying tropes, such as ritual, exchange, magic, etc. So even though these classic tropes are no longer very active in themselves, they are sometimes a resource for moving into terrains of the modern, the rational, and the contemporary, especially in the West. If you go beyond that or work differently, then you are doing something unusual and therefore you are not necessarily criticized, you can even get a reward for that, but the work is insignificant, the work is . . .

PR: Invisible.

GM: Yes, invisible.

TR: How to change that?

GM: Well, what is at stake, and needed, is the forging of frames, techniques, and practices that are deeply anthropological but don't have to depend on such "signifying" tendencies, the clever uses of such tropes. Marilyn Strathern is perhaps the great and artful current practitioner of this bridging of, say, the anthropology of new technologies and the concept of the person in specific Melanesian societies.[16] The question is what is anthropology itself going to do about these complex and substantial receptions of its research, already out there, so to speak, and in relation to which its own internal, guild reception, while authoritative, is often anemic—neither of profound nor lasting impact. So, perhaps this means that anthropologists will have to theorize and create norms for these present conditions of reception within their own models and expectations for standard research.

DIALOGUE III ANTHROPOLOGY TODAY

FRAGMENTATION AND MULTIPLE DISCOURSE COMMUNITIES

T R : We've discussed how the norms and forms of traditional ethnographic work—i.e., a focus on far-away places, ordinary people, culture, etc.— continue to implicitly organize mainstream anthropology. However, much as some anthropology may have changed, mutated, and adapted, such newer types of anthropology are perceived somehow as not fully anthropological. What is needed, then, are bridges that connect past and present anthropology. If this does not happen, George, are you suggesting the discipline might disintegrate?

G M : Well, anthropology is not on the verge of disintegration. Institutional inertia alone will keep it going for some time. More significantly, anthropology has useful and important things to teach the world, but much more pressing is what it has to teach itself. Is there a coherent answer to this question? Are the previous renovations of the ideas and styles of inquiry in the study of culture sufficient to revitalize anthropology's own intellectual culture? I confess to a primary, even emotional, concern with the relative prestige of the discipline—how it is received, understood, or listened to by those who fund it, by its publics who seek to learn something from it, by the disciplines to which it has related and with which it has formed sustained collaborations, and, perhaps most importantly, by the very subjects of its field research. Much more than ever before, subjects have to understand what the project of anthropology is and how it relates to their own interests and lives in order for them to be effective partners, informants, and subjects in our agendas of inquiry. So understandings of reception today are inseparable from constituting the very data that ethnography distinctively generates.

PR: So you're seeing real fragmentation and multiple discourse communities who share very little but some implicit sense of what an anthropological project of research is.

GM: Or the haunting of the notion of what constitutes anthropological research by regulative ideas still very much in operation.

TR: The classical norms and forms?

GM: Yes, as I have tried to sketch, the topics are gone but the norms and forms, at the level of practice, still exercise decisive control over what anthropologists listen to, don't listen to, and can think about as anthropologists. This is not "policing" in the highly negative sense, but deeply internalized, self-selected desires of anthropologists committed to a distinguishing research practice that, far from being outmoded, is enjoying new respect and caché.

TR: So there is a need for an explicit reflection about these norms and forms, a kind of making them visible and debatable.

GM: Yes, but that is lonely work. There are a lot of us who have thrived by doing productive things in interdisciplinary arenas where anthropology enjoys a certain intellectual distinction, but who don't particularly care about the state of the disciplinary community. The question, "What is anthropology now?"—an inward-turning interest in revising disciplinary agendas as such—does not necessarily propel movement toward the frontiers of the field. In fact, to answer such a question could be an obstacle or a distraction. In any case, many successful anthropologists today care little for reestablishing a disciplinary intellectual center of gravity. Many might even think that it is no longer possible to do so or not even worth doing. On the other hand, Paul, you are definitely not one who takes for granted, or has given up on the question, what anthropology is, or what it might become, within its own disciplinary frame.

PR: No, but I am a hyperactive pessimist, to use Foucault's phrase,[1] about the actual existing discipline. My hope is focused on the future, on students, and on respondents who send e-mails from Iran or Peru.

GM: I think it is of the utmost importance to keep arguing about the purely internal, disciplinary tendencies of anthropology, despite the difficulty of so doing. Solutions to the problems of reception and the ephemerality of substantial ethnographic work depend on finding intellectual centers of gravity for its diverse and centrifugal research participations, even if these participations are not the centers of gravity right now. They should be reappropriated into a disciplinary discourse of some sort. A range of prominent anthropologists are addressing the character and substance of this future disciplinary discourse.

JF: I agree. I think that one sees this quite vividly in the recent editorial projects of such journals as *American Ethnologist* or *Anthropological Quarterly* or, in Europe, *Social Anthropology*.

GM: For me it is the most interesting meta-theoretical issue right now. Paul has moved beyond his *Writing Culture* affiliation but I am still very much identified with that moment. When I give talks, I still speak in the shadow of its legacies, of what people have made of it as time has passed.

CHALLENGE: CONTINUITY ACROSS CHANGE

TR: George, one of your criticisms of contemporary anthropology is that today anthropological work is nearly always first and foremost ethical and political but often only secondarily analytical. Can you identify anthropological projects that are informed by politics and ethics but which are first of all analytic in their orientations—work that takes place in new arenas and is therefore no longer reducible to the classical norms and forms?

GM: It's not hard to identify such work. You find it especially in engagements with the sciences, with markets and finance, with the circulation of art, with the media. The problem isn't that it doesn't exist, but that it tends not to have very much disciplinary reach.

TR: So the challenge consists in creating a space for such work within the anthropological discourse, to create the conditions of the possibility that this work would be recognized as anthropological.

GM: The distinction between the ontological and the epistemological, which Jim mentioned earlier, is helpful here.

TR: You mean on the one hand a focus on the fieldwork scene, on encounters with people, on the organization of fieldwork and on the other a focus on objects, rationalities, institutions, i.e., on the things to be known, right?

GM: Yes. If you focus on the ontological, you have to do a kind of conceptual work that will be accessible and adoptable. People might appreciate Paul's concepts as developed in *Anthropos Today*—and even use them among students and with colleagues. But in the current fragmented nature of anthropology, would such a conceptual scheme have much of a chance in the discipline at large? I take Paul's work to be moving in this direction—ethnography as a project of conceptual work—but fieldwork needs to be re-functioned from its traditional formation as method in anthropology radically enough so that the discipline fashions new terms that replace "ethnography," "fieldwork," and "culture." In my own efforts, in partnership with Doug Holmes, we remain true to the norms and forms regarding method that still haunt the discipline. For example, we are interested in what has happened to "the native point of view" and the changing nature of fieldwork and its persistent Malinowskian scene of encounter. Our engagement is more aligned with the existing professional culture of anthropology, which is mostly concerned with epistemological issues. So in evoking terms like "para-ethnography"[2] (what the contemporary "native" might offer the anthropologist as "point of view") or "imaginaries" (what anthropologists work inside of so as to create a map or design for fieldwork), we retain some of the terms and contours of traditional method in order to refashion it. Paul, on the other hand, starts elsewhere to do this job of reform, which makes the task of communicating a design for re-functioning more difficult than ours, more estranging to anthropologists. What Paul is attempting is more radical and perhaps richer conceptually.

JF: Could concern for the epistemological—the tools ethnographers have available to produce anthropological knowledge—and the ontological—

the development of new tools for studying new objects, in a way that could potentially create a space for new work to be viewed as anthropological—be brought together?

GM: An analysis of these two different concerns could be important for reestablishing the standing of anthropology in its diverse environments today, to counter the dangers of invisibility, ephemerality, and the powerful stereotypes that anthropology has long left behind in its practice.

JF: I agree. Epistemologically, anthropologists are obliged to remain critically vigilant of their ontological commitments. But the exercise of such vigilance can't have as its result an anthropology that is devoid of or somehow beyond ontological commitments. We always do and always must have such commitments—revised or refigured as need or obligation arises.

TR: So, in a way, the challenge is to have a sense of continuity despite all the changes taking place. Hence the task is to relate new forms and concepts to the traditional *mise-en-scène* of fieldwork. The focus on fieldwork then could provide a bridging between what we've been referring to as the epistemological and the ontological.

GM: I think so, and I am grateful to Paul for proposing something completely different, so to speak—an alternative in another key or set of terms, one that boldly works in a frame different from "fieldwork" and "ethnography" but that still encompasses their tradition of practice in anthropology. To think differently, we need difference, and the schema of conceptual tools such as "equipment," "problematization," "apparatus," "assemblage," "event," the "untimely," the "actual," and so forth provides this.[3] Whether one agrees or not with the results, no one else who is as deeply in touch with the tradition of method in anthropology has done this so radically and systematically. Yet, in the end, to communicate such an alternative scheme, some sort of translation is necessary back into the terms and expectations of anthropology, such as the cultural, or culture, which you, Paul, are not really interested in describing or analyzing.

PR: I came into this discipline when it was still a numerically small field; its horizons were very broad and many of its practitioners styled themselves as bohemian. Stanley Diamond,[4] for example, would regale me with all the poets the field had known and their ardent politics. I approached anthropology as one among several disciplines that could contribute to an understanding of the larger world. It is the larger world that mainly interests me, although at the same time I have always thought that method was important. I have done a large amount of fieldwork in the last fifteen years, but since I have not been primarily interested in the mainstream preoccupations of the profession—identity politics, or the (re)discovery of colonialism, or the deconstruction of science—I have had to forge my own path. I have always remained loyal to a vision of anthropology by remaining vigilantly disloyal to the existing state of affairs.

GM: But you are not interested in what has long been understood as "a native point of view," even the recent reformulations of which presume the holistic analysis or description of a systematic cultural model or logic expressed in practice. Yet, a concern for this form—from which an ethnographer is expected to present rich materials and data from fieldwork—would enable you to establish a crucial connection to something that anthropologists have thought much about. Not losing this continuity is important. I might add that I dislike the term "native," or "native point of view," which was a caricature even when Geertz appropriated it into his discussions of interpretation.[5]

PR: I agree that making connections is essential, and I think the project that we're engaged in here, at some level, is precisely to make some of those connections visible for emergent anthropologies elsewhere. So let me offer one, in the form of a thought on description. *A Machine to Make a Future*, my Celera Diagnostics book, is a kind of writing degree zero. It is a modernist project where I wanted to be utterly saturated with things I know and to disappear from the text. But in some ways that form of modernism is now traditional—it is hardly new. On the other hand, the project rejoins anthropology by demanding an engagement with the unfamiliar. However, whereas no one would ever say to Marilyn Strathern, "The fact that you're making us learn these terms from New Guinea is illegitimate," they will say that about a SNP [single nucleotide polymorphism]. I don't know what to do about that except persevere. Why is there such an investment in refusing to be open to the contemporary world? In a very different mode, I am attempting a version of Hans Blumenberg's attempt to articulate *The Legitimacy of the Modern Age*[6] for the contemporary—or to be mindful of Foucault's comments that the opponents and critics of modernity have been all too frequently counter-moderns. Having said that, I suppose what it means to be consistently "anti-contemporary" is worth exploring.

GM: I heard you refer just now, if obliquely, to the near dogmatic practice after the 1980s of putting yourself in the text. Writing oneself into one's work became synonymous with being reflexive, but even though sometimes creatively practiced, more often today, the self-reflexive in ethnography (a near requirement) answers to a very narrow set of rationales and justifications.

PR: Getting rid of an embedded form of the subject so as to transform it into something more appropriate for thought and action is even more work than inscribing the self. And that's the work that I'm currently engaged in. These experiments can take the form of writing differently *and/or* the form of organizing collaborative research and writing such that the production of anthropological work takes a different form and has different norms than traditional ethnographic work.

GM: It was only inscribing the self that was canonized. "Where's yourself in this?" has become a cloying question. Becoming invisible, especially, now requires crafting, and is not getting rid of identity.

PR: It certainly isn't. It's a different form. And it's a move away from subjectivity to objectivity but it's completely rooted in a hermeneutics of the subject, which is a critical aesthetic, ethical, and even ontological practice, an undertaking of self-examination, of coming to terms with who you are and how you got to be that way that, if not done, leaves you with the naïve or debased or ill-prepared subject that you very likely are at the outset of any research project. Without this ascetic work on the self, one can't advance knowledge in our disciplines. The analytic work is hard enough to imagine and to practice; if one insists on an ethical dimension of care of the self, or others, and of things, then the challenge is exponentially more challenging and more worthwhile.

GM: For me, a key problem to address is how to establish "standard" works that can become exemplars for what aspiring, entering scholars should attempt. We all want to encourage work that can produce innovation, but there is a drive these days to create only singular works that will set the trend in a research area that is seen as new or emerging. Such high stakes burden the field—one either performs with highly exceptional distinction or one fails—since most of these attempts to be singular are bound to be ephemeral. There is little detailed examination of a range of new work by a disciplinary community no longer used to carefully consuming its own products of knowledge. The ethnography is more an aesthetic exercise, certainly not as subject to detailed reception and assessment, as it moves—theoretically, anyhow, it seems—into a comparative archive. Even if anthropologists are still reading, they're no longer bothering thoroughly to digest one another. This high-stakes game is unfortunate because anthropologists have invested considerable hope for their discipline's future in it.

JF: That's to say that it constitutes a mode of investing in the discipline's future that tends to exacerbate the disciplinary fragmentation that already exists.

TR: Which leads us back to the absence of commonly shared norms and forms in anthropology that would tacitly organize its "politics of knowledge."

GM: That's the problem, yes.

PR: So the point is to find ways to take conceptual work, put it to work in a practice of fieldwork, and then link that back to some kind of ongoing self-critical tradition.

GM: Yes.

PR: That it is your task, George, as an anthropologist of anthropology, to point toward such problems, to indicate where people get stuck with a game of form that is not productive.

GM: Maybe, though any discipline, including anthropology, only likes to hear in public about what's positive or progressive. I think I am doing that, if with a critical bent. One sees progress as working through knots and vulnerabilities.

PR: And hence it is a matter of debate. We should detect the implicit and under-recognized changes in the organization of fieldwork and method and make these changes explicit. That would be one quite big step toward changing the norms and forms.

JF: There are notable recent steps in this direction. I'm thinking in particular of the essays collected in Vered Amit's *Constructing the Field*.[7]

GM: To me, the character of anthropology as a challenged discipline is much more fascinating today than in the *Writing Culture* era. The experimental context of the 1980s has shifted now to the work of apprentices becoming professionals. From the point of view of current pedagogy—what is on the minds of mentors and students as they work through dissertation projects and how they might play out—the discipline seems to me in a moment of considerable ferment.

DIALOGUE IV THE ANTHROPOLOGY OF THE
CONTEMPORARY

T R : What is distinctly anthropological when anthropologists no longer study ethnos, culture, or society, when what is being studied instead are contemporary events and processes?

G M : When you talk about the contemporary, you strip anthropology of its former privilege of being out of time, and without immediately moving it to the more usual solution of historicizing the subjects of ethnography. Temporalizing is thus a key problem for ethnography. How to slow things down, but not be belated, how to avoid all too easy historicization that makes what is happening in the time of ethnography all too dependent on a past.

P R : What the present or the actual is is really up for grabs. As you say, the move toward historicizing the subject, or perhaps doing the "history of the present" can make valuable contributions but it actually takes us away from the practices that are making a difference yesterday, today, and to-morrow. As we have no philosophy of history or over-arching theory to guide us, the obligation to stay close to practices, to work hard at identifying significance poses a constant challenge. Certainly, the work of uncovering the contingencies of the present and their genealogical lines can be very helpful, and it is one reason among others that I am certain that collaborative work is a necessity. But I am not convinced that historical work is the primary arena or method for a future anthropology.

GM: But to speak of the contemporary is a provocation and we need to be clear about what we mean by it. I hear you rejecting any dependency on historical contextualization of what is going on in the present. Isn't this presentist? Aren't you asking us to forget history? Who can agree with that? And, in addition, there's a hierarchy of people talking about the contemporary—consultants, advisers to policy makers, etc.—for whom there are rewards of status and influence; being an expert is to talk authoritatively about what is happening in the contemporary world. What does an anthropologist have to add to what they are saying about the contemporary?

PR: George, the idea that I am eliminating historical conditions as partially determinative of the present is far from my position. All of my books have a historical dimension to them. The question is rather, as Nietzsche saw long ago, whether historical conditions are everything. And I believe strongly that they are not. There is a great deal of contingency and under determination in most situations. That being said, retrospectively one can always create narratives about what happened that are plausible.

Take, for example, the fall of the Soviet Union, the rise of the Internet, or genome sequencing projects. In the early stages of these events all of the experts were speaking authoritatively about the present, and what they had to say proved not to be illuminating. The Kremlinologists missed the fall of the Soviet Union; Bill Gates was very late on the significance of the Internet; we heard very serious debates about imminent eugenics as soon as the human genome was sequenced. That's fine, there's nothing wrong with being wrong; it is the essence of recursive and critical work in science. Niklas Luhmann makes the point that the function of experts today is to establish points of discourse and discussion, not to produce knowledge, and I agree with him.[1] Experts establish talking points in think tanks and at fancy conferences. Who ever looks back to discuss seriously the predictions and pronouncements? In contrast, the conceptual work of anthropologists is more lonely and isolated. Few journalists offer analyses at odds with the conventional wisdom. This is not to denigrate those first-rate journalists—quite the contrary—who have much to teach us about timely writing, investigation techniques, navigating the world of mass media, and the rest. Still, I don't think that anthropology is doing the same thing, or at least should be doing the same thing. Speaking to existing publics, in a language they already believe they understand, or that editors think they understand, is a fact of life for journalists. We should not forget that journalism is a method of policing new ideas as well. We have a duty, it seems to me, not to be always already accessible.

TR: Let's go back to the use of the term "contemporary." What does the term mean, for example, when one speaks about an anthropology of the contemporary?

PR: First, in a very unspecific way, that anthropologists work on phenomena that are characteristic of or give shape to the here and now. Taken as such the contemporary is a vague term. It just means that you work on something that is generally perceived as important.

GM: But the terms for analyzing what's important are always already given. You always work with given concepts.

TR: Yes, for example, by good and investigative journalism. I understand that this is one of your main concerns. For on this level there is little difference between, for example, journalism and anthropology.

GM: Right. That's the problem with drawing too stark a divide between the accessibility of the journalist and the "inaccessibility" of the anthropologist. None of us are de novo.

TR: But that's why it is important to make comprehensible the technical meaning of the term "contemporary," which is absent from journalism. Can you say something about this technical sense, Paul?

PR: The ordinary English language meaning of the term "the contemporary" is existing or occurring at, or dating from, the same period of time as something or somebody else, but it also carries the meaning of being distinctively modern in style as in "a variety of favorite contemporary styles." The first definition has no historical connotations, only temporal ones; Thucydides was the contemporary of Pericles, just as Thelonious Monk was the contemporary of John Coltrane. The second definition, however, does carry a historical connotation and a curious one that can be used to both equate and differentiate the contemporary from the modern. It is that marking that is pertinent to the project at hand.[2]

TR : Can you explain that? Can you say more on the relation between the contemporary and the modern?

PR : Just as one can take up the "modern" as an ethos and not a period, one can take it up as a moving ratio rather than a perspective. In that light, tradition and modernity are not opposed but paired; "tradition is a moving image of the past, it is opposed not to modernity but to alienation."[3] The contemporary is a moving image of modernity, moving through the recent past and near future in a space that gauges modernity as an ethos already becoming historical. The contemporary is not especially concerned with "the new" or with distinguishing itself from tradition. Rather, its practitioners draw attention to the distinction modern/contemporary as the clustered elements and configurations of the modern are observed in the process of declusterings and reconfigurations. The "contemporary" indicates a mode of historicity whose scale is relatively modest and whose scope is relatively short in range. Within that mode and observed from the actual, many types of objects are made available for analysis.

TR : So if I understand you correctly, the contemporary is a technical term that allows us to decompose emergent phenomena—for example, synthetic biology—into different elements that are assembled into one form constitutive of the phenomenon in question. Hence they are *con*temporary with one another. And the task of an anthropology of the contemporary is to choose—or find—an appropriate field site and to document and analyze such assemblages in the course of their emergence, to name them, to show their various effects and affects, and to thereby make them available for thought and critical reflection.

PR : Yes. The anthropologist of the contemporary has to be close to things when they happen but, by virtue of her analytical aim, preserves a certain critical distance, an adjacency, untimeliness.

THE UNTIMELY

GM : How is being adjacent connected to being untimely? What is the sensibility that defines these ways of engaging research?

PR: You have to produce untimeliness because you're engaged in *Wissenschaft*.[4] That's what we decided to do with our lives as intellectuals, as anthropologists.

GM: You mean anthropologists in the philosophical sense?

PR: No, not philosophical anthropology in the older sense, which is the pursuit of universal definitions of human nature or the essence of the human, but rather inquiry, anthropology in the vocational and scientific sense.

GM: Oh, anthropology in the vocational sense?

PR: Yes, whose loss you regret.

GM: Yes.

PR: And though I don't have any nostalgia for the older practices of anthropology (only a certain respect), I am trying to invent and practice an altered form that retains some elements of the old and adds some new ones. In that sense, the anthropology I am working on is "contemporary."

GM: But what again is untimeliness? How do we teach students to produce that?

PR: Well, I think that's a big question. The term is taken from Nietzsche's *Untimely Meditations* and used to mark a critical distance from the present that seeks to establish a relationship to the present different from reigning opinion. For example, the one thing journalists absolutely cannot do is be untimely. They work under severe genre and time constraints. Science journalists often take some time off to write a timely book (about the genome or the like) and then they have to go back to the *Wall Street Journal* or *New York Times* to earn a living. Such books are adamant about being "timely," "accessible," "instructive," and the best succeed in achieving their goal. We do not operate under the same system of constraints and rewards. We've always tried to teach students to think in a manner that leads to inquiry. We have given them concepts and methodological tools, which slow them down. Today, the pedagogic challenge is to rethink the established combination of fast and slow operations that remains at the core of what inquiry should be. One might say: "Let's go to Chernobyl, but don't leave Weber behind." Of course, Weber is not going to tell you directly what's going on there—that would be ridiculous to expect. But surfing the Internet is not going to tell you what is significant, either. For that we need other tools, other methods, and a different ethos. And hence a different sort of pedagogical work on the self and others from what we have pursued in the past.

GM: Where does this untimely work occur? Is it part and parcel of the exact same scene of fieldwork, or is it really something that unfolds elsewhere, say, in a scholastic sphere of considered debate and discussion? I think that this is an important issue because what happened after the 1980s was that everything that anthropologists thought and imagined became compressed within the mythic scene of fieldwork and writing ethnography, thus making both bear an intellectual weight that they were never intended to bear. Traditionally, the job of ethnography was far more self-consciously humble and limited, and it's very difficult to do at that. Personally, I'm glad that it became something more, but I'm also thinking now whether, in terms of the scheme or vision of research on the contemporary that you are devising, the theory-heavy ethnography that followed *Writing Culture* suits what you have in mind. With its additional load of developing theory, assessing the present, sustaining a kind of moral discourse, being inventive and original, and so forth, anthropological ethnography, as text, has become very little accountable to the data that comes from fieldwork—thus the complaint heard these days, often from older anthropologists, that "there is no ethnography in ethnography anymore." But it seems to me that the untimeliness you speak of is partly in accord with such criticism. It seems not only to call for a rethinking of "being" in fieldwork but also objecting to the pretensions and excesses of what has been made of ethnography after *Writing Culture*. And it does so in the absence of the sort of disciplinary reception that would hold ethnography in simpler times (when topics were more settled) accountable for its data. Untimeliness is a powerful accountability for where ethnography sets itself in real time, or outside it. It at least encourages a more rigorous setting of ethnography in relation to a particular set of relations or field of study.

PR: I think we're on to something here. Untimeliness perhaps was built into traditional anthropology through "the Other." You didn't have to worry about being timely because whatever you were doing was in the ethnographic present, a rather enduring temporality, even if, it now seems, an imaginary one. And the task then was to run it the other way—for the anthropologist to say, "You may think all of this ethnographic stuff is irrelevant but, you know, as Margaret Mead teaches us, we have a lot to learn from the Samoans about adolescence and sexuality. It is very timely." The arrow of relevance used to go that way but now we have to cultivate untimeliness and this runs precisely against the journalistic grain of being relevant immediately. It only happens if you do sustained inquiry. If the Weberian and Foucauldian question is the question of scientific and ethical asceticism—that is, what is the price to be paid for knowing?—the older response, which centered on claims to being able to establish ethnographic authority, is no longer adequate. And yet a sustained practice of the balancing of adjacency and immersion—it used to be called distance and intimacy—still haunts the discipline, as you have pointed out. And to a degree, I am also haunted. But not as the mystic is haunted but as someone engaged with one aspect of a larger methodology and life experience that must now be made more explicit so that it can be clarified, changed, and put to the test of experience and experiment.

FIELDWORK AND THE DISTINCTLY ANTHROPOLOGICAL

GM: The issue of the distinction or distinctiveness of anthropology as a knowledge practice was and is important, particularly now. Does anthropological research offer a distinctive sensibility about things that are already known or equivalently known in other discourses and disciplines of inquiry, or—and/or, really—does it generate distinctive kinds of data and results from them that really are not duplicated by other discourse or traditions of inquiry? Of course, both could be the case, but anthropology rose in the past primarily because it could provide the latter. It is not so clear that it has such distinctive specialization today; certainly, it has distinctive messages, structures of argument, even moral argument, and in this sense it may be most distinctive as a field of restatement, of revising arguments and debates in place. That is its distinction as rhetoric of cultural critique. Fine. But I think both you and I are not satisfied with just this. We believe that fieldwork/ethnography in the anthropological sensibility delivers both distinctive and novel materials, first, from knowing something different from what others know. Some may think it is too late to claim disciplinary boundaries as real and defensible—and it may be distasteful to champion distinction in this way—but operating in a disciplinary or even interdisciplinary structure requires the production of distinction to function. To implement the valuable critical sensibility of anthropology also requires, I believe, a basic, substantial distinctiveness in what it can deliver from research, all the way down to the level of reconstructing the nature and form of data on which ethnography depends. But this task begins with the course of conceptual work and innovation that you and, to a lesser extent, I have set out upon. Whether or not what we are proposing can reconstitute notions of what data are, it's a start.

PR: But I think it's already there in what we have been doing.

GM: But that it is there needs to be argued for and demonstrated explicitly, especially after a long period when anthropology's research agendas and analytic styles have become so blended with other discourses and practices. Its distinctiveness has been even more dependent on a certain emblematic tradition of inquiry and research practice, but even that has undergone considerable change that has not been articulated, as we have been discussing.

PR: It could be articulated, though. It seems to me the space to do it exists.

GM: Yes. The space to do it exists, but that's a special job. I don't think most people are keen to have such a discussion about method, on which so much hinges. I think they are happier to press on and let the classic method change incrementally, under the radar, so to speak, and leave the ideology of method, in which so much of the identity of anthropology is invested, alone.

PR: But undertaking that special job is what being untimely means. If such work were widely recognized, it wouldn't be untimely.

TR: We seem to always to return to the same point, namely the need to reconnect new research venues with the traditional or classical tropes of anthropology. The adjacent/untimely seems to offer such a connection insofar as it reminds us of the classical anthropological concept of "being foreign."

We've been somewhere else and now, coming back from there, we are sensitive to the peculiarities of our own culture or can describe it with the eyes of others.

GM: I am interested in how the untimely as a positioning is justified or expressed within the scene of fieldwork, among one's subjects and, indeed, patrons who facilitate one's presence in certain sites. And here, I am thinking of the diverse kinds of people with whom you have worked in recent projects, most of them being counterparts in some sense—experts, specialists in a different realm. How do you justify the untimely in that key space? Is it necessary that you do so, or is the untimely a concept mainly to be shared among "us," anthropologists or researchers who may be collaborating with you or who are simply interested in more cogent understandings of new moves and challenges in fieldwork? It is easy to imagine that you might be working with someone who doesn't care about untimeliness, is indifferent to it, or might even be hostile to it as an impediment—it encourages reflection when quickness may be what is needed among actors in the site of fieldwork. This is the issue that I have raised about the effect of slowing things down by the tempo of inquiry. Even if the situation is better in that there is real mutual understanding, or at least they, the subjects, may see the value of untimeliness in their midst, still, the intellectual or existential loneliness of taking such a stance, to which you have alluded, remains. Of course, such loneliness is nothing new in anthropology. It was produced in the space of the relation to the traditional informant on whom the anthropologist has depended, but who was likely to know or care little about his scholarly purposes. In your recent terrains of research, the stakes are much different, because it's not over there, it's here. The standing or reputation of anthropology itself, as a putative science among scientists, is in question and really matters in terms of the quality of the material and observations that you are able to develop in such terrains. This is fieldwork within modern knowledge forms and within the same communities of hierarchy, rewards, ambition and competitive evaluation. So the untimely is rooted in this resignation to being lonely that you express.

PR: Which anthropology has always had, after all.

GM: Yes, but with the realization or comfort that the anthropologist would be coming home eventually, and with the romantic idea, very strong in anthropology, that fieldwork seeks out community, which is absent or hard-won in modern life, and appreciates it whether or not the experience of fieldwork allows the anthropologist to partake of it. In your case, untimeliness is not situational in this way. It is a stance that pervades life within the bounds of fieldwork and outside it, more a condition of critical thought. But in fieldwork it comes up against people—often counterparts—trying to do things, and it is very unpredictable what the response to a posture of untimeliness generates, that is, if it is shared at all, rather than being a sort of background condition or contemplative state restricted to the fieldworker alone. So, I'm wondering how the untimely manifests itself in the scene of fieldwork as it has been traditionally or currently imagined, or how to think about the untimely in a rather literal way. Also, what is the relation of operating in the temporality of the untimely to doing "conceptual work" as the primary modality of research?

PR: The task is to invent concepts to make visible what is emerging. This needs a critical distance from the present, and this distance, at least in part, is achieved through the proper use of analytical tools.

GM: Where I may differ is that I purposely sustain a kind of literal-mindedness, always pulling back questions to what goes on in the transformed scenes of fieldwork today. This might be my limitation in relation to your project, but in the background I always have this pedagogical issue or purpose in mind: How are these ideas to be presented in usable forms to students who may think broadly, but in the end will have to fit their research into some acceptable present version of the anthropological culture of fieldwork? I am willing to play beyond this, even to entertain that we are on the verge of suggesting very alternative practices to the tradition, but ultimately I am pulled by this rather pragmatic concern. So, is the untimely, doing conceptual work, something that quite openly is done explicitly with reference to what used to be called "key informants," once "others," now more likely to be what I call counterparts, experts, scientists, journalists, anyone who comes to have real stakes in the work they are doing with you as anthropologists in their lives?

For myself, I see a lot of the alternatives Paul proposes for an anthropology of the contemporary as an interesting and necessary means with which to rethink the changing nature of the relationships of fieldwork in its complex, multi-sited terrains and politics.

Untimeliness is what really marks the anthropologist as different in a field full of competing and overlapping discourses and related purposes and projects. While it is a temporal term, untimeliness is what creates or imposes the space for the ethnographer in settings where that space of being or presence is otherwise hard to define and establish these days. It, along with other terms that you have introduced, creates a temporality in which anthropological research can function, in which it can claim novelty, discovery, in its knowledge-making—which is one of those aesthetic dimensions of anthropology that I claim will not be denied despite all the other changes in our practices. Just presenting the "stereotypic anthropologist," as generally understood, in such settings works against the relations the anthropologist needs to be able to function in contemporary research. The anthropologist must have a different, negotiated relationship with subjects as, to a degree, her epistemic partners. To accomplish this, sameness and difference between anthropologists and subjects becomes a key realm for rethinking method, practice, theory, etc. The terms and ideas that you have introduced to constitute an anthropology of the contemporary seem to facilitate these needed discussions, but I am not sure this is what you intend or care about.

PR: But pedagogy and *Bildung*[5] and their discontents and pleasures have always been center stage for me. It is the teaching and learning that keeps me alive amidst the torrent of endless petty politics, seemingly never-ending bureaucratic impediments, and pervasive ethos of academic ressentiment.[6] My effort to build a collaboratory is certainly pragmatic.[7] It is a space of adjacency, perhaps a heterotopic space, in which multiple people can work together in their differences. And it is generating multiple research projects of an exciting sort. There is nothing other-worldly about it. The work of *Wissensarbeitforschung*[8] is co-labor yielding labor and finished works.

GM: For me, the whole project of an anthropology of the contemporary—not just the data that it provides for manipulation, but its interpretations, the concepts it creates, and ultimately the critique that it is prepared to deliver to its publics—hangs upon what is going to come from these relations of fieldwork as epistemic partnerships/collaborations. You talk of adjacency. I talk of mutual appropriations in these relationships.[9] Both have something of the idea of contest or agonism about them. The anthropologist's purposes are different from his counterpart's in the field, and ultimately the partnership breaks up more or less congenially—the norms for producing scholarship are still highly individual, and results are primarily for the professional community and not that of subjects. But generative relationships in fieldwork are predicated on mutual purpose or usefulness. When the power relationships in the fieldwork situation are more balanced, or even reversed, as they often are nowadays, appropriation is not the bad word that it was in the postcolonial or neocolonial context of much traditional fieldwork.

TR: What is it that the anthropologist wants to appropriate?

GM: I would say a grounded and strategically elicited imaginary to work inside of as an ethnographer. The course or map of fieldwork has to be found within its confines. Such a found imaginary is not the end of research or its descriptive-analytic object, but its medium. Fieldwork can only function in this way where the traditional notion of entering into and working through another lifeworld entails forming relationships of mutual stakes and mutual appropriations for different purposes on a common intellectual ground, forged together in perhaps a halting, partial way, but sometimes, when one is lucky, in a committed way. This is the primary research context, I presume, for the conceptual work or labor of which you speak—orientation to a common object of present mutual curiosity, which is not present in the situation of fieldwork, but elsewhere.

TR: So the level on which you want to keep anthropology anthropological does not so much concern the objects of study, be it culture or society. What you care about are the relations between ethnographer and counterpart that are constitutive of fieldwork. Here we need reflection, because this is where ethnography, as a research process, takes place, and it is seems this is precisely what makes anthropology exciting for you.

GM: Yes, there's still something in the job of proper anthropological inquiry that many people don't recognize as being essential to any kind of adequate social or cultural inquiry into the contemporary. This is at the heart of Paul's criticism of a recent paper by Habermas in which he absorbs developments in the life sciences into his critical view—an exercise in him keeping up.[10] Habermas is sensitive to the contemporary but his responses to it rearticulate the critical positions that we have all heard before, and so the phenomenon coming into being suffers conceptual neglect. It is not explored in its own terms; predictable implications are drawn.

TR: Let me gloss you on this, George, and come back to the distinctively anthropological. For Habermas, the concepts we have and live with—life itself, reproduction, kinship, human dignity, etc.—are a given. They are sort of naturally there. For the anthropologist this is radically different. What anthropologists can do, because they analyze present events "as if" from afar, "as if" a lab were another culture, is to recognize contingencies where others see natural and necessary developments. And this allows one to have a different kind of conversation based on different kinds of sensibilities. Now how would you name this distinctively anthropological moment? It is not the exotic and it should not be the moralistic. Would the "foreign gaze" do? I.e., a kind of "foreignness" detached from the spatial connotation of the term?

GM: Well, the foreign for those who don't think there is anything or anyone out there to connect directly with. How about simply the located, or the particular (which is not necessarily a place or a community, but a multi-sited terrain, an assemblage), signaling the appropriation of the reflexively critical—or potentially so—out there ultimately for one's own distinct purposes? Even though the traditional way of constructing the exotic and foreign is gone in anthropology, unless you can produce something like that, and its effects, then you're not doing proper anthropology. But what is produced is not going to be the exotic, or even the foreign. Perhaps it is going to be the contemporary, insofar as the contemporary yields one or another dimension or aspect of otherness, which still is expected of anthropology and haunts its practice, but which is really in need of reconstruction and rearticulation.

PR: And the anthropology of the contemporary achieves this by asking what difference does today make with respect to yesterday—and to tomorrow.

The focus is on the emergent, on that which cannot be adequately grasped with yesterday's concepts and ideas.

TR: Could one say that the distinctly anthropological evolves around a difference but this difference is neither spatial nor cultural but rather temporal?

PR: Yes, although it obviously is a matter of more than time. It is also a matter of a conceptual relationship to otherness and a distinctive engagement with a particular scale of historicity.

MAKING THE UNTIMELY AVAILABLE FOR TEACHING

GM: And this implies that distinctly anthropological inquiry provides something that other types of social and cultural analysis overlook. In saying that others overlook it, I'm indexing my interest in the uniqueness of anthropology and its role within the ecology of other discourses. I approach students today with the prod—tell me something I don't know or tell me something somebody else doesn't know. The anthropology of the contemporary operates between the desire for a reestablishment of the grounds of its intellectual distinction and the fact that it ultimately derives from—or, at most, supplies "value added" to—already existing, competing, or parallel discourses provided by the media, journalists, other scholars, or even the subjects themselves. Any anthropology of the contemporary is fated to be derivative in this way—to provide discussions of other discussions, to arrive belatedly and to stay longer. This is perhaps key to its temporal distinction, while still wanting to preserve relevance. But in trying to be distinctive while also being resigned to being derivative, anthropologists of the contemporary still want to have an answer to the question: "Look, reflexivity now exists in every discourse domain and site of fieldwork, and aren't you just telling me what 'they' already tell themselves, and perhaps the world? Aren't you just doing a translation for those who don't already know this, or might not have already heard it?" No, the anthropologist is not simply doing that, yet is indeed working derivatively, and has little choice but to depend on actors and their already constituted discursive realms. What you have to do these days to pursue successful fieldwork is to locate and construct partnerships—usually unstable—with technicians of general ideas, whom Paul first evoked in *French Modern*. We have to be sensitive to the kind of actor we're engaging. It's not enough to talk to just any scientist who will talk to you, in which case you are just collecting interviews.

P R : That's right.

G M : But it's the constructing of just these sorts of partnerships that no other discipline appreciates in the way that anthropology does—or, at the very least, can.

P R : That's why anthropology is untimely.

G M : But most anthropologists don't confront this, right?

P R : Right.

G M : And then you'll have further discussions, either with the people with whom you're working, or with others—and that's the best we can do. I'm saying this because I am afraid that anthropologists inquiring into the contemporary will be misrecognized not as untimely but as timely. There will be a strong inclination to read us not in terms of what we say about the accuracy of *our subjects'* anticipations but in terms of the accuracy, or acuity, or persuasiveness of *our* anticipations. My point is that we're designing in some way the terms for new norms, forms, and expectations for ethnography as we reset its conditions. And I want to be understood— agreed with or not. Mostly, I don't want to be lonely.

P R : I don't think you have any choice in the matter. We're talking about the ascetics of knowledge, the price to be paid for a certain type of practice.

G M : You provide promising conceptual resources for actually doing this kind of distinctly anthropological inquiry in the contemporary world. But we have to do more than this. We have to make it effective for students. They need a set of operations or frames to help them recognize this dimension of emergence and actualization in the always unruly and incoherent process of talking to people in fieldwork.

T R : George, is the epistemological continuity that you are concerned with— i.e., the effort to keep anthropology anthropological on the level of fieldwork encounters—also the key for understanding the concepts you have come up with in recent years, such as paraethnography, complicity, epistemic partners, and above all, multi-sited fieldwork?[11]

GM: I think we need to make the effort to articulate an intelligible relationship between the concepts we provide for an ethnography of the contemporary and those concepts that have been definitive of ethnography as it has long been known. What I have in mind, however, by the "paraethnographic" corrects an approach to the design of fieldwork that flows from a now conventional and too literal understanding of multi-sitedness as simply following objective processes out there by some strategy. Multi-sitedness designates a kind of path of movement in fieldwork, but where does the path come from? A wall chart? A diagram? A map? A blueprint? A course for ethnography set by some influential macro-narrative of process of how capitalism works? Of what global process is? In introducing the concept of the paraethnographic I mean to point to a different practice that more directly relates to how fieldwork evolves these days as an engagement with found imaginaries,[12] and a literal exploration of these imaginaries as a framework for ethnography. I suppose this is an account of how some of Paul's key terms like "apparatus" and "assemblage" arise through reconceived but still quite traditional understandings of fieldwork. Much depends on the strategy by which one selects a center of gravity, the found imaginary, which is going to define the purview of a project. This found imaginary could begin anywhere—with experts, or migrant workers—and eventually these sites or positions will be connected if they are relevant to each other. Sometimes the ethnographer defines this relevance as her argument and makes connections between overlapping worlds that may only be indirectly perceived by the actors/subjects, or not at all. It is not only the native's point of view that is operative.

TR: So behind your idea of a multi-sited fieldwork stands your effort to emphasize the emergent quality of ethnographic knowledge, almost in the sense of a logic of discovery, a discovery of connections, and this practice can only evolve circumstantially, namely in the nitty-gritty arena of fieldwork, in encounters with local others.

GM: I admit to a certain mechanical character in articulating this preferred mode of evolving a complex, multi-sited field of research. In its initial awkwardness, it reminds me of a Rube Goldberg machine. It's a design for a kind of contraption. This contraption is the working construction of the ethnographer, but it is untimely. You develop this design as you find yourself in situated engagements with epistemic partners, but you are constructing it for your own purposes, which are those of making the tools, the concepts that permit the exploration of the kinds of relations that a distinctive anthropology of the contemporary approaches. Theoretically this process could begin anywhere, and in anthropology it usually begins in the communities of the marginal, the ordinary, the everyday, and the subaltern. But I do think it makes a difference if you begin in an expert or elite context. The danger, though, is that you will not move beyond that context. Elites can be involving, beguiling, intellectually challenging, but, in my view, they are finally only resources for defining a course of multi-sited fieldwork, and that course may or may not end with them as the object of analysis or critique. Much work in anthropology has taken this form in recent years, but there is no explicit articulation for working in this way specific to the ethnographic tradition. That is what I think your conceptualization of the anthropology of the contemporary offers.

DIALOGUE V IN SEARCH OF (NEW) NORMS AND FORMS

FROM EXPERTS TO THE ORDINARY

TR: I want to begin with a brief summary of what we have already said. George declared that what we are doing here is discussing the possibilities for norms and forms of anthropology, norms and forms here understood in the plural and open, that we are exploring the possibilities for a basic equipment, or basic equipments, that would set the standard for anthropological work today. Such an equipment is first of all concerned with keeping anthropology anthropological and hence would imply the primacy of fieldwork and analysis over theory and ethical and political commitment. George, who tried to capture this with the concept of multi-sited fieldwork, repeatedly described Paul's work, with its focus on the emergent, the actual, in a word on the untimely, as a promising and advanced equipment for anthropology today. One recurrent question though was whether the applicability of Paul's equipment is restricted to work in certain arenas with certain actors, namely technicians of general ideas, or whether it could be adapted—and changed—to different arenas. The background of this question was George's observation that traditional epistemology of anthropology was designed for a focus on the low rather than on the high, on the ordinary rather than on the event. Maybe we could talk about that?

PR: The concepts I've used in my most recent work have been forged in relation to a specific venue. Could one take this approach, for example, with migrant workers? And I don't see why not, although I think there are some differences in orientation and organization that would be interesting to explore.

GM: An issue arises here that I would call the "modulation of tempos." In research the anthropologist is often operating in a different tempo of conceptual labor from that of her subjects or counterparts, and that this marks a big difference in purpose, interest, deciding what ideas are important to develop, and so forth. The anthropologist generally wants to slow her expert counterpart down, but the subaltern subject generally wants to slow the anthropologist down. Now, these differing tempos are not a big problem if your fieldwork is "out of time," but if your fieldwork is conceived in terms of temporal distinctiveness—as with some of the terms we've been discussing such as the untimely, the timely, the actual, the emergent—then the differences of tempo within a fieldwork relationship are a crucial dimension of fieldwork to analyze. This manipulation of time, the timely, of temporality, is, I think, absolutely a key way to address the question of whether your concepts could be developed among those who are not experts, scientists, intellectuals, and so forth.

PR: Do you want to start there?

GM: Maybe. I am trying to clarify whether this scheme (or contraption, in my case) that we are developing here has specific, limited application or whether we can make more general claims for it. It is inevitable that when you suggest a scheme, an alternative frame for thinking about method, it will be received, at least by some, as a "one-size-fits-all" model or form, with general applicability to any subjects. It can be applied, for example, to any subjects, potentially—peasants, workers, as much as experts and scientists. Work such as yours begins in realms of expertise but doesn't necessarily have to end there. Research is completed by a movement beyond the initial milieu of study to some other relevant sphere or spheres that have been entailed by the first. One does fieldwork in the field of the imaginary of the first and eventually brings it back there. So there's a movement away from and back, and that's the movement of critique, in which your purpose in continuing discussions with your first, orienting subjects is to bring the reality of something that's in their calculus back to their discussions. Suddenly you're no longer in the proverbial role of fieldworker as learner, or marginal native, but you establish a different role—the anthropologist with her own, probing, questioning agenda, exposed to subjects. And that's an independent, even slightly aggressive act. They may like it, they may not like it.

TR: Let me translate this: That's your epistemological or encounter-based account of what you call Paul's object-centered or ontological work, namely his analytical focus. Your epistemological idea of multi-sited fieldwork, methodologically speaking, is closely related to Paul's object-centered ideas of assemblages and apparatuses. So there is a certain compatibility between your approaches.

GM: And exploring this fit or compatibility between our concerns is a very worthwhile way to respond to the need we each strongly feel to rearticulate what research is today from our shared personal histories with anthropology's highly emblematic culture of method through a striking period of change. But, proceeding a little further with the implication of my contraption for practice, it's in the act of moving beyond orienting encounters—say, with experts, scientists, and technicians of general ideas—and in the return to them from elsewhere with the news of the realities that your original informants only imagine or presume in their own milieus, ethnographic research gains a certain critical dynamic, develops material for the critique that it wants to make. Interpersonally, the result can be an atmosphere of betrayal, or one of discovery—they disappoint you, you disappoint them maybe—but finally you are pursuing your own analytic agenda, still in the confines of fieldwork, and no longer just studying their culture or practices as resident anthropologist.

PR: Yes, so it's a combination of fieldwork, conceptual work, and collaborative work.

GM: Yes, that's good. This agenda comes to the anthropologist by working laboriously through a particular embedded imaginary, which I would say, given my sense of ethnography as a humble act, provides all the good things that anthropology can offer. But the key point is that all of this work, in some ways, needs another operation, and that operation is a literal movement to another site that's intimately—or, imaginarily—connected to the first. Your own orientation in this kind of work is definitely expert- and elite-based. Here, your recent *A Machine to Make a Future* is apt. What I like about this book is the success you have in getting the actors at a major biotechnology company to talk at length and with subtlety not only about their own world of work but also about implication, about how what they do touches seen and unseen constituencies, publics, agencies, and ordinary people. Although your account depicts the intense locality of the surroundings at Celera, the reference of much of your informants' discourse is to the person "out there" who expects something from what they do—perfect material with which to launch a multi-sited design.

PR: That's right. One could very easily make that move.

GM: So I'm thinking about what imaginary dimensions of situated research would or would not allow the ethnographer to continue on her own with critique in mind.

PR: Let me push you on that.

GM: When you move on from the elite, expert, or intellectual milieu to the scenes of ordinary life imagined or referenced in their discourses, it seems possible to me that you will remain within the compass of the expert imaginaries with which your research began. Now you could logically begin the other way—establish the imaginaries of, say, migrant workers and then move literally into the sites of elites, experts, or more privileged others that they evoke. If only because migrant workers are well-known subjects of ethnography and elites are not, I think it is far more likely that if initiated among migrant workers, the alternative that we are trying to clarify between us would wind up being about their culture—it would be pulled in this conventional direction—rather than about the contemporary. When you begin with experts, there is no tradition of studying their culture. Milieu, scripts, what the data might be are all less predictable. For this and other reasons, the research paradigm that we are arguing for seems destined to be immersed, at the beginning, in some realm of collaborative effort, among experts, of knowledge-making.

PR: I am not sure I agree with that. What you mean, I think, is that at any research site you have to keep in mind that it extends in many different directions—more than any single research project could encompass. But imaginary, it seems to me, is too limited to encompass that complexity. It is confined to the mental lives of particular actors.

GM: What would be a better term?

PR: Your term contraption is actually a better term because it is less mental. It refers to a disjoined set or processes in the world that actors, perhaps including the anthropologist, are seeking to connect. But there is no overall strategy or plan guiding this motion.

GM: How does this relate to the notion of assemblage?

PR: Contraption is broader because to me assemblages are already centripetal, and your contraption idea, which I like, gives us some sense that a research design extends in lots of different directions. There are nodes and rhizomes at various points, but making connections to these things can never be fully accomplished because there isn't any whole to connect to. There isn't any unified culture. There isn't any underlying society in which you could get to the core or the essence. It's a bricolage, which is another form of contraption, right? So instead of imaginary, I would rather speak about vectors of power and force lines that you can't control. Imaginary is too mental for me.

GM: Imaginary, I agree, is a troublesome term in fairly promiscuous use today and needs to be made more precise. I'm happy to try. I am really not talking about an artistic or aesthetic imaginary or something of that sort.

PR: And it's not really a subjective term though it has that connotation. It's a grid of connections that are not just mental in nature.

GM: I yield for the purposes of our discussion here. I see exactly this move toward the ontological about which we have been speaking, but my own thinking still tends toward concepts that lend themselves to epistemological questions and process.

PR: With the people at Celera, we are dealing, at least in part, with *logos*. That is to say, I'm concentrating on experts, basically on people who are making truth claims. But there are plenty of other people whose lives are not centered around authorized truth claims and, therefore, *logos*, per se, is not what they're concerned about. To concentrate on their imaginary would be to limit oneself to only one part of their story. I'm ethically convinced and committed to the fact that if you go across the street and talk to any group of people, you're going to find reflective people there. The guys who work in the labs or the patients that Rayna Rapp studies are not themselves doing science—they're not technicians of general ideas—but they're reflective about their lives, and their lives are cut by these scientific or legal or financial vectors of truth claims.[1] So there are many ways to do research even in a lab not only focusing on technicians of general ideas or those concerned with *logos*.

GM: But scientists or experts are custom-made for your kind of questions, for your focus on the emergent, because scientists are discovering what human beings are, what the world is, what counts as reality.

PR: Yes, I am working with technicians of general ideas, but the work is not, at least not exclusively, about technicians of general ideas.

GM: We agree there. You're not trying to give an account just of their ideas because that would be the pursuit of describing their culture as primary object, to say, "Here's what they think." No, they already say what they think. Instead, you're actually taking these ideas forward for other purposes in the operation of research.

TR: Perhaps we only need to change our perspective in order to see that and why one could do an anthropology of the contemporary among migrant workers. Paul's work is focused on the emergent, and its privileged analytical objects are conceptual shifts and movements. Simply put, events change the way we think or can think about certain things, and the task is to identify and map such events by way of doing fieldwork. Hence it seems to me that Paul's work is not so much focused on truth claims as such but rather on events or actualizations that take place in a certain field, namely the field of the biosciences. And if one speaks about conceptual motion then things appear in a different light. The "mode of analysis"[2]—i.e., the focus on the emergent, on actualizations, on conceptual motion—works as well with migrant workers.

PR: I think that all that would be required is to shift attention away from migrant workers as a group defined by and expressing a pre-given social and cultural identity and instead to expand one's attention to migrant workers in relation to their defining attributes, namely "work" and "migration." And work and migration are related to economy and to politics and to technology, and to nation states and potentially to science. I see no inherent reason why such work should not be possible.

TR: Me neither, but George's point, if I understand correctly, is that the problem is to make this mode comprehensible or conceivable *as anthropological*. What is required, at least when we speak about concepts, is the kind of epistemological work George has been pointing to. For example, in your essay on holism in *Ethnography Through Thick and Thin*,[3] George, you show that for anthropologists there is more or less no escape from holism. You brilliantly describe an epistemological dilemma: Fieldwork was designed for the holistic study of cultures but we happen to no longer study "cultures" and thus the kind of totality so deeply inscribed into the culture concept—a concept that implicitly and tacitly still organizes the field—has become an obstacle for new research. If you work on migrant workers you need to say something about "the social" and their "culture." But if one is concerned with the emergent, with conceptual motion, then this is different. There is no whole—the culture of the migrant worker. What is actualized or emergent has nothing to do with whatever totality, but with the combination of different elements, hence with an assemblage, that creates new conjunctures that lead to new or at least different dynamics. It is circumstantial and in motion. Terms like migration, work, social, cultural, economy, nations are in flux and this flux—the concrete movements we're seeing today—are the object of analysis. And this requires fieldwork.

PR: I completely agree with that.

TR: So the question is: Can we change the deeply embedded epistemology of fieldwork that organizes research? How do we find ways to articulate, take into account, and make explicit this shift in mode, from a holistic approach, focused on the study of a culture, toward a contemporary approach focused on assemblages, problematizations, rationalities, and so forth? I think this question is what we are discussing here and where the two of you meet.

GM: Perhaps one way to get at this is through attention to discourse—as people talk about whatever, there are certain constructions or tropes that are recurrent and on which a certain discourse about the real world depends. And these people may be conscious of it, or they may not be. This is very old hat, but I do think we have to have some analytics here for what would qualify as ethnographic data. Because after we've theorized a new research paradigm, we're still asking students to accumulate what kind of data?

PR: Let me push that a little bit. It seems to me that this is one of the things that is wrong with the mainstream of science studies, one of its deficits. The sociological model and the literary-critical model essentially are interested in what they think of as theory, and then there are cases; theory is applied to a case. And this is, if you look at the modes of production, the reason Latour organizes things as he does; he earns his living and his students earn their living through short-term contracts—one- to three-month contracts—with the government or with business. So they developed methods whereby you can go and do a study of a complex organization in a month and write a long report. This mode of production is only possible if the theory is what drives it. And, so one of the things that I'm adamant about is that I am anti-theory and pro-concept and pro-experimentation.

GM: I sympathize with this, if I understand the way you are distinguishing theory from concept for effect—"doing theory" has become a specific kind of style that has come to have notable, unfortunate consequences for research, especially if you are trying to retain some of the virtues of ethnography, or at least, research in that tradition. We know a lot about theory. Yet, the ethnography is driven by a kind of openness to the perspective of others, but you have to have tools for getting at this, and we have to have conceptual tools, and we have to have analytic means. "Doing theory" in the contemporary style seems to get in the way of thinking through and within materials and data, and the exposure of theory in writing becomes the primary preoccupation of ethnography. I think we are here trying to preserve the virtue of thickness,[4] but without its traditional forms. So conceptual work—trying to provide conceptual tools to work within and through materials after the disappearance of the tropes, topics, and former tools—becomes a label for "doing theory" in ethnography.

PR: The reason ethnography—or, my preferred term, inquiry—needs to be thicker is partially because it's not localized in the way that either Geertz or Latour thinks it is, and partially because the contraption, the contrapuntal lines, are not something you know in advance. So you need to stay close to things; inquiry has to be "thick" because it's the only way you can find out what's going on. Otherwise, you know already what's going on and, therefore, ultimately you will not have done any inquiry.

GM: Yes. This is our frustration. This is the powerful thing that I think we share—that this thickness you're talking about is not made available or accessible in current work.

PR: This is where we converge, George. We both want to save something anthropological about this practice but it's neither thick description in the Geertzian sense, nor identity politics, nor deconstruction.

GM: No.

DESIGN STUDIO

TR: In your writings both of you have frequently mentioned the significance of pedagogy. I think the privileged place for solving the problem of "thinness"[5] could be a pedagogy that teaches how to do fieldwork. I am talking from the perspective of the student now. How to come to terms with fieldwork is really difficult. It is difficult to do fieldwork because you cannot know in advance how to do it and what you will find. You get to know people, you assemble notes, you do some interviews, etc. Your corpus of data grows but it is not at all clear what you should do with this data. One is literally drowned by the anecdotes, events, observations, encounters. The question is how to not be drowned—or how to be drowned while staying alert to what emerges. Theories or well-established forms provide orientation and hence a solution, but they often foreclose sensitivity to the singularity of a locality and thus the possibility of a genuine discovery.

The alternative, though—and I think here both of you agree—needs to be taught.

PR: This is what George's point is, if I hear him right. That what the anthropologist or the community, due to its shared sense of anthropological inquiry, is doing is intervening in an ongoing set of activities and practices. And the anthropologist needs to have a narrative form in which there's space for that to be part of what's being shown, and that's part of the complexity because it's also hard to have a voice when you are trying to solve a million other problems. So this is, back to one of the things that you have thematized so well, this is pedagogy. So this is back to questions of inquiry and pedagogy.

GM: That's good. Based on my experience supervising dissertations, I think they should be governed by a theorem of reasonable and responsible incompleteness, in which fieldwork self-consciously accomplishes something unfinished. The traditional "holistic" norms embedded in expectations of fieldwork can just pressure and overwhelm, long after anthropologists have given up the naïve, functionalist sense of the whole as totality. Also, I think the dissertation ideally should not be the first draft of a book, as it often is these days, but the opportune moment in which the research is completely accountable for the material that the anthropologist has been able to produce, messy as it might be. Theoretical, analytical originality, yes, but only in a close relation to "data."

There is quite a premium placed on the production of the singularly brilliant work out of apprentice fieldwork. It is unfortunate that the virtuoso style is fused with apprentice effort, and that so much rests career-wise in anthropology on this effort. I think we should be developing our ideas here not with "genius" work or performance in mind, but with the improvement of standard work, what is expected of any dissertation research of reasonable quality. The key question in defining standard work, given an ideology of high originality, is how to develop conditions for its collective reception other than in terms of the aesthetics of a brilliant performance. With this purpose of making research produced under an ideology of singularity subject to a standard of detailed, collective, and critical reception, I have gravitated toward thinking about the pedagogy of apprentice fieldwork/ethnography in terms of a studio or design practice—a process more characteristic of the arts than the social sciences, or, better yet, something in between. My own experience of this has been as a participant in architectural design studios and their programmed, stage-by-stage critical reviews of student work. The architectural student is supposed to produce something original, exemplary, personally brilliant, but accountable to a standard that gets transacted in the design process with its reviews. The idea of research design might be a good term in the name of which we could explore the pedagogical side and, in a sense, concretize the various ideas for alternatives in the conduct of ethnographic research that we have been approaching so far in our discussions.

PR: Yes, I think design is a good term.

GM: This idea of a design process de-centers the significance and weight of the fieldwork process conventionally viewed and makes it more organic and balanced with what occurs before and after it as part of research, particularly what occurs before, since, according to my contraption, so much of the activity of fieldwork depends on being able to construct the site or sites beforehand in a deeply informed, even ethnographic, way. This fashioning of the site in advance is something that seeing research as a design process encourages us to think about. The whole issue of a design process goes back to the contemporary condition we have discussed in which the ethnographer, to be original or distinctive, is required to enter the conventional scene of fieldwork today belatedly[6] and derivatively—and thus much better informed about how fieldwork is to be situated, at least initially, and what it can ultimately deliver.

PR: Yes, but you also don't locate yourself in the infinity of knowledge. For example, the head of the lab where Tobias sought to do research told him, "I'll take you in if you do this course in neuro-pharmacology," which seemed to me appropriate. We must establish conditions so that we can design this experiment in a plausible way whereby I can be assured that you're going to know enough to know technically what is taking place. It may be analogous to asking, do you speak enough Arabic? I think design is a word we ought to preserve.

GM: The design studio is a way to develop alternative ideas about method in a more comprehensive way than traditional attitudes have permitted.

PR: It includes and authorizes criticism as well, which is another one of the themes that we need to think about.

GM: Well, critique in design studios can be practiced to the point of vacuity and obnoxiousness, but, at its best, group critiques of projects work through materials and operative concepts at different stages as thought experiments and scenarios with various consultants in the room (including users, clients, etc.). Actually, I see something like this emerging in current projects with the aid of the Internet—students create blogs associated with their fieldwork, which are sort of a virtual design studio. But there are no norms or authority for this device. Aside from these halting efforts, there really is nothing in anthropology like the sort of design practices that are well-instituted in other disciplines.

PR: Yes. The sciences have such a technology. As you say, certainly architecture does, among other art fields, but the human sciences don't.

GM: And anthropology is the perfect one to have one.

PR: Right. Because it's close to practice. It is itself practice-oriented. It's not theory-driven, so there are embodied skills involved. What we lack, therefore, is a space of criticism, but one in which there is authority as in the lab meeting or in the design studio. And there's plenty of authority and power in anthropology, but it's not given a function, it is not focused and it doesn't move.

GM: And this could be the space, in the domain of pedagogy, where the disciplinary discourse and community of reception in anthropology can pragmatically reestablish itself. Rather than hoping for it through new exemplary ethnographies with more interest, new twists, and brilliant performance, we could look for renewal through this process and not through the final exam that the ethnography has become.

PR: We could also look toward making the solitude of anthropological research additive, because isn't it now time for anthropology to move beyond single-person projects? Recognizing that careers are still individual, there could nonetheless be ways to work collectively in this design space that would facilitate everybody.

GM: Yes. Anybody can be in the room in a design studio.

PR: So it would be a shared space, a cooperative and collaborative intellectual space. Because there is not one unique common project, there is a need for the challenge of collaboration, one constituted by a shared sense of norms and forms and a common interest in design. The result would be a back-and-forth, a recursive shaping of each other. And such a design studio would have a strong dimension of ethical and analytical work.

TR: So, the design studio is not organized by a planning rationality, where there's a single authority on top, sitting there, drawing a map, telling the students what they have to do. Instead it's collaborative, in a mode designed to facilitate the process of invention, of learning, of analysis.

PR: And anthropology would seem to be particularly well-suited to this type of activity because of the traditional dimensions that we each have our own autonomous domain of experience, one tribe, one island, and so forth. Consequently everyone has a degree of autonomy, authority as well as the ability to contribute something specific to a larger project. The danger in anthropology, therefore, is not homogeneity. The danger is not having anything in common except a mythos of fieldwork.

GM: Yes, and that's what I am concerned about. Brilliance is great, but sustaining a sense of, and conditions for, standard work, is better—a more pressing challenge. I mean, everybody should be of a certain ability but that's not even the discussion.

Work by immensely influential figures such as Bruno Latour and Donna Haraway circulates inspirationally, but their personal styles of brilliance, with which so much of what they offer is tied up, cannot be reproduced by students even if they are extraordinarily able. My concern is not about brilliance.

PR: It's about high quality work.

TO MOVE BEYOND THE ESTABLISHED

GM: It's about high quality work that's accountable to a community of people who question it, who settle it into a sense of common project. Most books that we get now from younger anthropologists are ones that they produce under pressure of tenure requirements. They have to write them to succeed in academia, and they have to write them according to the fashions that have defined certain orthodoxies and rhetorics since the 1980s. These are determining of the shape of ethnography—models of originality, singularity, critical virtue, and so forth. The ethnography or anthropological monograph has gone far beyond its once rather modest role (which of course had its own orthodoxies) to a form that showcases brilliance in theoretical acuity, storytelling, and the power of selected material and key metaphors. The current forms of what is expected of published work by new talent are dictated by certain senior exemplars, that shape them definitively, but by which they also seem, too much so, copies. It is sometimes difficult to distinguish what precisely is being moved along or ahead in new work—building a store of knowledge, an aesthetics of style, or both.

PR: The older exemplary monographs form inappropriate models for the contemporary problems.

GM: Yes. I think the issue generally is that ethnography in this present state very problematically serves its traditional, crucial pedagogical role in anthropological training for research. Of course, ethnographies serve other constituencies, and they must be read and assessed individually, but if you realize pedagogy through the idea of a design studio that we have discussed, this would have eventual implications for the form of ethnography, or even its status as the sole genre form bearing the weight of much anthropological discourse. This one-size-fits-all genre is badly in need of change, but it can't be legislated by a *Writing Culture* sort of critique or showing of alternative textual strategies, glossed as experiment. This just leads to the problem of exemplars. But, I don't think the monograph as we have known it would survive the design studio. Ultimately, such a process would encourage different forms that now get meshed and categorized in the revised conventions of genre writing after the 1980s. Anthropological writing, in my view, needs a lot more recognized diversity outside the hegemonic ethnography rubric. A design process would bring this needed therapy about. To be sure, current exemplary ethnographies make interesting reading—and offer important thought—but they are a clumsy instrument for teaching what research is becoming and might be. And it might also help, as well, to relieve the present crisis of publishers in putting out genre ethnographies for very limited readerships.

PR: But I do think the outlines of such alternatives are already legible in a number of new works by younger anthropologists and they are well worth reading for pedagogical purposes. So I think we have some idea and some movement forward.

GM: I agree that works in the current form have the elements of alternative within them. Take, for example, two recent works, operating in the same general terrain of environmentalism and justice, that of Adriana Petryna's *Life Exposed* and Kim Fortun's *Advocacy after Bhopal*.[7] Each in its own way is deeply engaged and struggling with the limits of form to take on problems of unusual dimensions. These are problems of scale and temporality, which are not only challenges to analytic forms, but also to forms of inquiry and the composition of results—let alone of the venerable ethnographic textual form. Of the two works, Petryna's book still retains the traces of a common post-1980s form for ethnography while Fortun's does not. But the latter pays for this in a certain messiness, a certain "bursting at the seams."

TR: So the point you are making is that Petryna is reproducing and working within an already existing form?

GM: It's a work of impressive scope, but still written from the point of view of a particular set of clients, patients, sufferers, citizens of an independent Ukraine. It builds a remarkable range but it remains within the frame of the usual subjects. How she manages this is well worth studying for reading back into fieldwork strategies relevant for many contemporary projects. But what constitutes ethnographic material—thick analysis or description—remains conventional, excellent but conventional. Fortun's book is not definable in terms of what gives Petryna's anchorage. It might have been had it remained tied to the original site of ethnography, activism among disaster victims in Bhopal. But the unusual dimensions of Fortun's book, and how she situates herself ethnographically within them, reflect a real wrestling with temporal issues, many of them circumstantial and unanticipated. Fortun came to Bhopal belatedly, after the disaster, but just in time for advocacy. The result was successful—a true experiment by circumstance. Fortun's book reminds me of Gregory Bateson's *Naven*, that long-standing classic on an obscure piece of Melanesian exotica, which has sustained enduring interest precisely because of its nature as an accidental or found experiment in the design of ethnography as research practice and text.[8] Like Bateson, Fortun flirts with a project that might spin out of control but succeeds in finding creative solutions to sustaining coherence. By no means, however, is her work an exemplar or model for dissertations. Its potential influence, like that of *Naven*, is in addressing questions of designing fieldwork and writing around new senses of problem for ethnography, but far from remaining idiosyncratic around traditional topics. Perhaps, most important for us, Fortun's project—the book as well as the research that led to it—is driven by efforts to find solutions in practice for the complex issues of managing temporalities which threaten to outrun her project. These are precisely the problems that are so distinctively fascinating in trying to articulate an anthropology of the contemporary. In fact, I think she actually came up with a temporal posture that exemplifies what we have been calling here untimeliness.

TR: So she submitted to the field and found the design while doing fieldwork, a kind of extension of the design studio to the field. And your point is that pedagogy in the form of the design studio would, if successful, provide such a transition to the field?

PR: Well, there are many different ways of relating to and thinking about the present.

TR: Yes, we need a multitude of design studios, so that students become familiar with a whole range of possible designs. That could move us beyond scripts.

PR: See, George, I think there's potential, but the potential lies ahead. Foucault made that wonderful remark—"'we' must not be previous to the question."[9] We need to make a future "we" possible rather than asserting an already pre-formed identity to which one demonstrates loyalty and fealty.

GM: So there is a critical element of thinking through this based on a pedagogical innovation.

PR: I think we should push that.

GM: For me, there is this question that I intimated when discussing Adriana's and Kim's books, about whether you can develop such innovations if you begin and stay with the usual subjects. If you do so, the scripts for writing ethnography, in the current era, are already predetermined.

PR: I see what you're saying. So, you want to disrupt them?

GM: For us, in what we are trying to do in our work now, these scripts are far too narrow and limiting. So while in solidarity with their ethos, aesthetics, and commitments, we are trying to develop alternatives to them. It has probably been easier to do so in anthropology's entry into science studies because these encourage, even require new scripts, yet unformed, so to speak. To put my finger on it more directly, this terrain or arena often requires the ethnographer to deal with the science (experts, elites, policy-making circles) before the people, or to deal with the people through the science. You can see this in the work of such exemplars as Latour, Haraway, even Strathern. But I want to understand the anthropology of the contemporary more generically, within the tradition of anthropology—its ethos, aesthetics, commitments, and the range of topics in which it has been interested, especially from its so-called Golden Age through the perceived waning of this high period.

Actually, after the 1980s, the typical script of ethnography was about the "resistance and accommodation" of common people, the marginalized, the disadvantaged in the face of world-historical and systemic forces and their effects in everyday lives. And there was a lot of hope and nobility in this terrain—it instilled anthropologists and others who pursued this trend of scholarship with a virtual politics within their work and it aligned sympathies with NGOs and with social movements. By the late 1990s and early 2000s, after the energy of academic interdisciplinary movements had waned as well, the same scripts for ethnography in anthropology took a darker, less hopeful turn. "Resistance" in its local and emerging transnational forms gave ground to the study of more desperate situations and predicaments—refugees, the diseased, the slaughtered. Powerful critiques of the state and international forms of governing are being delivered by ethnography in this way. And the sort of work that we are thinking through here is not at all incompatible with what the post-1980s scripts for ethnography are producing in anthropology, but we are beginning from somewhere else, and the figure of ordinary life does not have the same valence in our schemes. In my view, the present scripts, because of the traditional commitments of ethnography that imbue them, can never quite get at, in equally ethnographic or anthropological terms, the systems, processes, or regimes of knowledge that permeate every site of fieldwork. This is what we are trying to get at as ethnographers of the contemporary, while being true to the historic commitments and aesthetics of anthropology.

PR: Yes, I agree.

TR: Okay, let me try to rephrase this. So we're saying that implicit in *Writing Culture* were assumptions about ethnographic work and these assumptions continue implicitly to organize anthropological work. These assumptions function as a script. Anthropology is about ordinary people, about victims, sufferers, the view from below, and so forth. One organizing element of this script is that analysis is secondary to politics, right? So what the design studio would do is it would break such scripts by making them available for thought and this would open up the possibility to move beyond them and to pay a different kind of attention to the material at hand.

GM: Right.

PR: What you're saying about scripts is helpful. Consider the ethics of ordinary life, that is, what people consider the good life to be. The other day I was in Emeryville, a town near Berkeley. Next to the Trader Joe's, there was a sale going on at the Sprint store. There were seventy-five people in that store. What is the image of dignity, of self, and of worth that's going on there? To begin by analyzing them as dupes of capitalism is the wrong way to begin. This is not to say that they're not being manipulated, but we could say that about every group everywhere. There's nothing distinctive in saying that. The forms that would be appropriate to studying that group of shoppers would be different from the forms used to study scientists at Celera, but it could be done. There are moral voices among the shoppers at the Emeryville shopping center, and they would be self-reflective, too.

GM: This reminds me of the tension between distinction and derivativeness that characterizes anthropological research today. The anthropological tradition, no matter how much we might want to change it, provides something that is being missed or not articulated by other types of scholarship. Anthropology is not merely representing the consciousness and thought of ordinary people, but we are actually saying things that are novel, and that are gotten at empirically. This is our proposition because if you're not going to study the Trobriand Islanders, and you're going to work in the realm of the presumed familiar, you're going to find things that are not radically different necessarily but that are just otherwise unavailable. And we find our own way to a distinctive 'found' expression of known or commonly understood problems of the day by listening to other people as our subjects and being accountable to that process as our primary form of data. But, however anthropology reinvents its classic distinction of discovering what is overlooked, marginalized, or suppressed within new schemes like the anthropology of the contemporary, it does so inevitably by being derivative, by covering ground that others—the media, other disciplines, the "natives" themselves—have already represented, written about, described and analyzed. Probably what separates us most from scripts in place is that they are still deployed with the assumption that anthropology can have its distinctiveness without paying attention to its derivativeness. We want to take this problem on squarely. We are trying to design techniques, equipment for research, which face up to anthropology's present condition of distinction and derivativeness, and the tension between the two.

PR: That's right.

GM: I think we agree that we are not merely reinventing methods for a special subject or subject position, but rather for a different set of conditions that redefine research itself—its boundaries and purposes. So, in terms of the categories of the present scripts, we must take on the challenge or at least the questions of defining the place of the usual subject, ordinary people, in our scheme and not leave it to a division of labor, as in: we here are defining method for a 'special' case or subject only of ethnography that has been traditionally marginal—elites—leaving the study of ordinary people

DIALOGUE VI OF TIMING AND TEXTS

THE TEMPORALITIES OF FIELDWORK

TR: A theme that has frequently surfaced is the significance of fieldwork-based inquiry, the absolute importance of stationary, long-term field research. Both of you agree—and insist—that it's out of fieldwork that anthropological knowledge emerges. And yet, you thoroughly reconceptualize the practice of fieldwork. Usually, fieldwork is assumed to be focused on things social or on things cultural. For you, though, fieldwork is no longer predominantly about people and hence "society" or "culture" but about temporal processes, e.g., the emergence of forms of rationalities, of institutions, of assemblages. This brings me to what I think of as crucial in our effort to build bridges: the need to spell out this link between fieldwork and a focus on the temporalities of its subjects and objects. What would fieldwork focus on and how to conceptualize that focus? And what consequences has this for anthropological conceptions of thickness or of ethnographic data?

PR: And what consequences does this have for the form writing takes? I would like to return to the question of form and writing and the impact a focus on the contemporary has on the ethnographic monograph as we know it.

JF: We could consider the relationship between the "anthropology of the contemporary" and three categories—not just the category of the emergent but the other two that Raymond Williams develops in *Marxism and Literature*,[1] the residual and the dominant, arguing that they are always constitutive of the present as a dynamic phenomenon. I know that for you, George, Williams is an important reference.

GM: Yes, in a way I think that an ethnography should ideally address of all these categories and their conjunctural relation through any particular concatenation of sites. And I would say that what fieldwork virtually alone can yield is the three in play, and their configuration.

TR: I think a focus on the contemporary could do this. I mean, take the term assemblage. An assemblage consists of different elements with different temporal trajectories and different contexts of origin. So in order to understand any contemporary phenomenon one would have to decompose it, make visible its elements and their diverse temporal trajectory.

JF: One can imagine several ways of relating to the triad. It seems to me that what I do as a habit in my own research is actually to focus on the residual and the dominant and the violence of their contemporary relation more than the emergent, per se. That it is to say that I tend to frame my projects in such a way that the emergent is a derivative of the residual and the dominant and the violence of their relation.[2] That just seems to me to be a framing issue. I think it's one kind of perspective on the present that one can take whereas one can also focus on events as generative themselves and you get a different kind of text. You get a different kind of picture as a result.

PR: And a different temporality of research and of its textualization.

JF: And there are different possible frames. In its focus on the strategies of boundary-crossing exercised by state-hopping elites, much of the recent work on trans-nationalism effectively treats the dominant and does it quite adequately on the basis of short-term engagements in the field. A few weeks really will do on many occasions. Yet, to give us the payoff of what I think to be the most incisive of theoretical claims of such work, that status systems are always local and that being transnational means integrating oneself into a plurality of them, for that the investigator is going to have to linger in the field long enough to explore the full substance of the status systems in question—quite a lot longer than a few weeks. One would have to settle in for a long time because those systems involve the residual, the dominant, and the emergent all at the same time.

TR: But even though you're interested in a timely anthropology that can produce results quickly that's not what you're doing, right?

PR: No, for sure. I would like to say two things. First, it is important to distinguish between Williams's concept of the "emergent" from an "event." An event would involve all three levels, the emergent, the residual, and the dominant. And second, yes, I agree with Jim. I think that the attention to micro-practices and/or everyday life is extremely important, because it demands a time commitment and there's no way to rush everyday life. To do anthropology it takes a long time to figure out what is significant about what is going on, because what's going on is not obvious and often not quite what is being talked about explicitly. Although at times people do know what they are doing and can talk about it quite eloquently. Identifying what is significant can't be done quickly, it seems, or at least there is no rapid means of guaranteeing that one is correct in one's assessment. Attention to the micro-practices slows you down, so let's slow down.

GM: I agree. And I think to get at these micro-practices is what distinguishes anthropology from the other social sciences. Fieldwork does not just consist in taking interviews. It consists just as much in attending to the unspoken.

PR: There is a sense that there are residues and unexpected qualities and long-term, tacit familiarities that are in the sites and circuits that fieldwork inhabits and we're the only discipline that gets at them. That being said, I don't think most anthropologists actually do that well.

JF: I don't think most anthropologists do it well, either. In part because it's really hard and being a good anthropologist really is invariably much slower than the usual grants now permit us to be.

TR: But Paul wants to speed up anthropological inquiry, right?

PR: Well, if anthropology is to remain pertinent to the contemporary world it *must* figure out how to speed up certain aspects of its practices of inquiry. Certain of the venues we come to are changing too quickly to allow us to do anything else.

JF: Yes, but only certain aspects. Others remain in need always of more sustained, inferential, and indirect attention. And that's a matter of "unbearable slowness" because, indeed, it is hard to do; it would take a long time to capture that dynamic in the field and then in a text—virtually by definition.

PR: I would like to return to the question of form and writing and the impact a focus on the contemporary has on the ethnographic monograph as we know it. For you, George, a wonderful ethnography would have the emergent, the residual, and the dominant in it. How would such a wonderful ethnography look? And what kind of authority would be attached to it?

JF: You may object to the characterization, George, but for you I think it's supposed to look like a Thomas Pynchon novel.[3] George is waiting for the realization of the paranoid ethnography.

GM: (laughs)

PR: But fieldwork can't do that.

JF: Well, fieldwork alone cannot generate the material for such a text, but fieldwork combined with archival, secondary kinds of research could. The paranoiac's imagination—in which everything is connected to everything else, every "here" to an "elsewhere"—is the textuality proper to the paranoid ethnography. We had a graduate student at Rice, Jamer Hunt,[4] who was very intrigued with Michael Taussig's essays on paranoia as method in *The Nervous System*[5] and Dalí's "critical paranoid method,"[6] especially as Rem Koolhaas applied it in *Delirious New York*.[7] In these he found powerful manifestos for the exquisite attentiveness that one might hope that, as an anthropologist, one brings to one's work.

GM: I was excited about Jamer's analysis because this was in a way what I had had in mind—that you walk around with your eyes way too wide open seeing all kinds of connectedness near and far, imagining the present as a tissue of impingements from near and far. That's what I'd like to see in the ideal ethnographic text—and that's why being a good anthropologist is, again, so unbearably slow.

JF: So the question of textuality remains.

GM: As do questions of representation. So, in that respect, it's not right to say that *Writing Culture* is somehow dissipated or has altogether lost its productivity as a device for generating questions.

JF: We are still "writing culture"—or in any event, still writing in relation to it, whether directly or obliquely, whether for it or against it.

TR: I am not convinced. I would prefer to say that some of the concerns that have been central to *Writing Culture*, especially the question of how to construct a text, are still with us—but that today these challenges appear in a fairly different form. The key issue is no longer "representation," or writing "culture," no?

PR: When we talk about what's left of the power of *Writing Culture*—my view is that the question of the form that writing takes is still very much on the agenda. And my view is that there should be multiple forms and that there isn't going to be a single form that's going to be adequate. But maybe it's more of a goal for you, George—the monograph or what would it look like?

DESIGNS FOUND IN THE FIELD

GM: Well, I would like to take the emphasis off the monograph as we have known it. Monographs are more interesting as symptoms or indices of transformation and change. The form itself is bound to change further, perhaps even go out of existence, given the present contexts of publishing and new information technologies. Therefore, in fact, I would like to take the emphasis in our discussion here away from the monograph as we have known it and focus once again on the state of reflexivity in anthropology—not on reflexivity in the writing of ethnographies but in the inevitable stories or shoptalk that one tells in the confines of professional culture. These sorts of stories have been very important in instilling method in anthropology, and they must still be today. But we should listen for those stories that are no longer so much about the fieldwork experience bounded by the Malinowskian scene of encounter, but more broadly about the design of research. Such stories would come to evidence, I suppose, a fascination with the sort of contraption that different courses of research become these days in unfolding. This is still all very individualistic in the manner of tale-telling, but that is still the predominant form of research experience in anthropology. So ironically, after exhaustion with so many years of tales of the field, more tales are exactly what we need—at least for a while longer—but that deliver different sorts of accounts. In effect, we do not yet have the design studio that we have been imagining, but we still need the designs, and these can be had by telling different sorts of tales of research, tales that have the contraption in mind that research in and on the contemporary has become. I believe these different sorts of tales are being told now, especially by younger scholars and by students in areas such as science and technology studies but by no means limited to it.

PR: What would such a tale look like?

GM: Such stories should be very specific and individual because we need to know what's going on out there that is not being articulated within conventional fieldwork frameworks. Experience is an important guide here for producing thinking about new forms more generally. For example, in our previous discussions,[8] I outlined a preferred way of developing multisited ethnography, differing from, or more particular than, my general proposal for it, and certainly differing from the way it was taken up. It was inspired by my original reading of Paul Willis's *Learning to Labour*, reflected in my own contribution to *Writing Culture*,[9] and by certain turns that my research on dynastic families was taking. My tale of research goes like this: In the early 1980s, I began the study of wealthy capitalist dynasties with the study of families—their relationships, their kinship, their habits of consumption—as the taken-for-granted primary subjects of ethnographers—similar to how historians and a variety of social scientists had established a literature on this topic. I came to see that these families, in their most motivated and even intimate relations, were the work of wealth and its complex technologies of increase, of distribution, of image management, of care. But what was this wealth as an ethnographic object in comparison to the family that was its dependent or, shall we say, it's wholly owned subsidiary? Was wealth only gray men and women in bank trust departments to whom the beneficiaries would go to ask for their ancestral benefits? Hardly. Neither their wealth nor they in relation to it could be conceived in such dormant terms. Anyhow, where was the center of analytic, ethnographic gravity in these parallel structures, of a very different character, but complexly entwined? Moreover, I challenged myself to prefer wealth over the family as a primary object of ethnography, thus entering into the sort of part technology, part social environments of fieldwork that are often encountered today. This specific fieldwork challenge stimulated an early appreciation of the issues of multi-sited ethnography and of the role of human subjects and sites in the conjuring of assemblages, apparatuses, etc. This experience, reinforced by a line of reading, plus the need to teach research to students—who came to graduate work inspired by the interdisciplinary period of theory and wanting to do something else with the traditional fieldwork modality—spurred me to make something more generic of the challenge of the fieldwork on wealth and families. Out of my dynastic wealth research, I had the uneasy sense that tales of fieldwork are stories you can tell your colleagues, students, and professors, but that they are not really stories that you should be telling alone, by yourself.

I want to emphasize the utility at the moment of such tales, since I think a lot of the productive thinking going on now at the theoretical or conceptual level comes from very specific research experiences for which old tales of fieldwork don't fit. This seems to be true of you, Paul, I think, and of Marilyn Strathern, Anna Tsing,[10] and others. Personal struggles with fieldwork tradition and research conditions produce more general visions of method that arise from these particularities.

TR: I found what you have been saying very illuminating. I mean, you basically introduced us to your laboratory of thoughts, the conjuncture of work on elites, a care about ethnography, an effort to develop it further as an analytical tool. This shows just one more time that the characterization of you as anthropologist of anthropologists is not adequate or at least not exhaustive. Your idea of multi-sited fieldwork was articulated with regard to the work you cited in your review article, but if I understand you correctly, it grew essentially out of your own work on elites. The idea was to imagine a kind of anthropological method adequate to a theme as complex as elites, which cannot be grasped with the scripts available. So multi-sitedness is your methodological effort to break the script inherent in *Writing Culture*. It is your effort to bring the ordinary and the experts together in one research project, the high and the low. Or said temporally, the residual, the emergent, and the dominant. And in addition you're emphasizing the primacy of the research process, the need to discover the relations between these different domains.

CASUISTRY AND PARTIAL KNOWLEDGE

PR: Here's a question I want to ask. When you say you have a preferred contraption or model, do you mean that at some point in your career and reading, there was something like an exemplar that seemed more or less right? Or do you mean that you've only seen bits and pieces of this in other people's work?

GM: Bits and pieces.

PR: And you still have a hope or a desire in any case that this could be done?

GM: Yes. But it could only be done by a reformation of pedagogy.

PR: Because?

GM: Graduate training is based on exemplars—reading ethnographies—but, as we have discussed, ethnographies are anything but exemplars today. Rather, they are to be read as experiments, for their bits and pieces. The best classroom discussions of ethnographies today that I have heard operate in this way, but then again, in such teaching/learning environments, the ethnographies themselves bear less weight in teaching method and research than they traditionally have. Again, I have the imagined design studio that we discussed in mind as an alternative.

TR: But you said you have a concrete model in mind. Can you say something about that?

GM: I do, actually, have a model in mind. But I've never spelled it out for anyone because it's very schematic, and it comes from my own research experience which I have just recounted. However, everything I've thought has in some ways been in terms of this model. What interests me is figuring out how, if you wanted to train students to do the kind of work we're talking about, would you have to train them differently?

TR: I want to push this point a bit because I think we can arrive here at another connection point between past and future. Again it seems to me as if the way you frame the problem is—if implicitly—in the form of a drama. You think that there cannot really be a general exemplar and in any case you don't want to declare a new exemplar because this would be dogmatic. You would name the new paradigm but you do not want that, because (a) this would result in a script, and (b) you know that anthropology can never produce such a universal paradigm because everyone has his or her tribe, so to speak. And yet anthropologists, as you emphasize, dream of such an ideal ethnography.

GM: Well, I don't dream of ideal ethnography. Not to do so was one of the things I took away from the *Writing Culture* critique. Henceforth, you would not get prototypes, or exemplars, but techniques, strategies, moves that could be thought through and adapted to one's own purposes. Unfortunately, anthropologists expected the new ethnography, the new exemplar, and it never came. It is not surprising, since the institutional factors that govern professional success—producing distinctive ethnographies, which is what publishers compete for—are on the side of exemplars, striving for the ideal ethnography. I consider this unfortunate, and I am more interested in what the standard form, or rather forms, of not *the* ethnography but ethnographic writing might be. I want to remove the weight that is given to the ideal ethnography, which is the primary form of knowledge that anthropology has produced past and present. I don't want to do away with ethnography, but morph it, not by rethinking writing strategies as in the 1980s, but by beginning further back with rethinking the entire research paradigm, which is what I think we are getting to here—by reconceiving the space, time, and operations of fieldwork; by rethinking pedagogy in the name of design; and by calling for some "ideal," so to speak, of standard work rather than exemplary work. This is what will eventually change the product. Ethnographic writing remains, but the aura of the ethnographic text enshrined by anthropological tradition is inevitably reduced in these broader reconsiderations. But until then we do have the exemplary ethnography as the primary form that we can best read, as many do, for its bits and pieces that are intentionally experimental or reflect the perturbing conditions of research that are indicators of the changes we have in mind.

TR: No, you don't dream of the ideal exemplar, but according to your diagnosis many anthropologists do. Today, just like after *Writing Culture*, they wait for "the" new work, which provides orientation. But, as you say, it cannot come. And this is what I called tragic, for there is no way out.

GM: Okay.

TR: And one way to do away with this tragic sense—and this is another epistemological shift that allows to build bridges—is provided by casuistry and case thinking, as Paul showed in *Anthropos Today*.[11]

PR: Yes, "exemplar" is a term that was central in casuistry, which before it got a bad name basically amounted to reasoning by appeal to relevant precedents, relevant analogous cases. The opposite of casuistry, insofar as it is case- or exemplar-based, would be a one-size-fits-all model.

TR: And that's precisely the predicament you're framing and in which you locate anthropology right now. People want a system but at the same time there can only be cases.

GM: A very interesting turn. Casuistry with its dependence on cases provides a very suggestive way to think about the almost fetishistic importance of *the* ethnography as the primary form of ethnographic knowledge. The frustration is that much of the intellectual ambition written into ethnographic texts these days remains unseen by constituencies who understand them primarily as case studies, as empiricist reports on certain particulars, as a modest form of truth-telling. Evoking casuistry here—which seems to me a bold move, since in common parlance it is often associated with dogmatic, clerical thinking—provides a different way to think of the value of case studies, as a type, for which the production of exemplars has significance in itself. Casuistry creates discourse by staying with and involution back in on cases. Reference to casuistry is a way to upgrade the ethnography as a complex form, as it has become. The alternative is to argue for the demise of the ethnography. A more diverse array of genres and forms of writing and publication would join it, or take its place. We would thus no longer be defending the ethnography as a case and, in turn, its exemplars, or else such a defense would be less important amid other alternatives. So we have two interesting options here.

PR: This goes back to questions of form. If the idea of the great monograph was to do a comprehensive account that brought the dominant, the residual, and the emergent into fullness and into relation with each other, that's either a dream or a nightmare. However, to keep them all present seems to be fruitful in terms of saying what it is that anthropology as a practice has to contribute. So cultural studies is interested in the emergent; political scientists are interested in the dominant; and anthropology is interested in the residual as well. The triad seems to structure a set of complex temporalities that we need to make choices about and that we can't forget. So if we forget about the dominant power, we're wasting our time. If we forget about residual, we're wasting our time. If we think it's all static and there's nothing emergent, we're wasting our time. Maybe you can't do all of them together. I am not sure. It seems worth discussing more.

GM : But the space of ethnography would bring them all together, no?

PR : Well, it depends on what we called the design of the ethnography, and this design depends on the singular circumstances of research and the shared questions and problems that define a design studio or a discipline. And so, as a discipline, anthropology should not be defined by an ideal book but by its method and by a common set of questions and a shared but intrinsically open set of problems, which allows for many different projects, designs, and exemplars.

DIALOGUE VII   DESIGNS FOR AN ANTHROPOLOGY
OF THE CONTEMPORARY

A DEPAROCHIALIZED SPACE

TR: This is our final session. It would be nice if we could bring some of the elements we talked about together in a coherent fashion. I think a frame for this could perhaps be provided by what we called deparochialization. I think it can do that because a deparochialized discipline is a diverse, heterogeneous discipline, impossible to reduce to one or a few key paradigms. It is open and vivid and moving.

GM: Yes, our generation are the ones who succeeded and never grew up in the sense that what the *Writing Culture* critique really did was to undermine the usual kind of professional authority that one could normally enjoy with success and recognition in one's research. Rather, it made the work that one was trained to do profoundly unsatisfying. So there was a prolonged adolescence of being the student, which in some ways was an exciting state to be in. But it made the orientation of people who gained quite powerful positions, who became the professors, disinclined to work with graduate students in the traditional ways. Many wanted a graduate student primarily and immediately as a kind of colleague, who has and is responsible for her own project from its very inception. This was probably always a dimension of graduate training in anthropology, but I think it has come to take precedence in our generation and after, over the sort of authority position professors are supposed to grow into. The whole model of mentorship in graduate training has significantly changed.

So you have major figures now in mid- to late-career who have achieved the status and material rewards of senior position—named chairs, large grants, directing centers and departments, etc.—who, quite openly, are still searching personally for a certain intellectual maturity. For example, anthropological studies of globalization—a major topic of research fashion of the era—by now should have been exemplified by collective projects, formal or informal, produced by the new senior figures as frameworks in which the research of students and up-and-coming scholars could flourish. But instead of exemplars in this broad research arena coming in this form, they still mostly emerge as single, usually very personal works—as ethnographies, sort of—or essay collections, or even semi-*mémoires* produced by the present stratum of distinguished professors. If you think of the "great figures" in the anthropology of the Golden Age, Eric Wolf, David Schneider, Marshal Sahlins, but distinctively not Clifford Geertz in this context, these were people who cultivated students to carry on in a way, and they have, in their own way. But there is nobody even remotely like that any more.

CULTURE AND THE CULTURAL

TR : In a certain way the disappearance of these father figures corresponds, if I may say so, with the denigration of the culture concept. Throughout our conversations we have frequently touched on the question of culture and its role in anthropology. We all agree that the time of cultural wholes, of separate islands of culture which anthropologists study, is more or less over. And yet, it seems that we're all dedicated in one way or another to culture.

JF : I would like to introduce a distinction between culture and the cultural.[1] We're content to do away with cultures, those bounded wholes. But we're not, I think, content to do away with the cultural, as a constitutive dimension of human life, as one of the planes—an open plane, to be sure—of which it is always composed.

GM : The cultural still needs to be addressed semiotically, since the cultural as a plane is made up of elements distinctly susceptible to semiotic analysis and diagnosis—tropes, discursive genres, rhetorical moods and rhetorical effects, orienting schemes, and systems of presumptions.

JF: For sure—I'm not content to do away with it, either. So when, for example, one encounters Bruno Latour's actor-network theory, there is the anxiety that everybody is going to get on Latour's bandwagon and that then there'll be no anthropology—or only a crude and trite anthropology—left. Because it's all about resource management and the objects thus managed, and culture becomes absorbed into the idea of technicity and reduced to the idea of technicity. This issue also provides something of a motive for preserving the term ethnography that's more than just inertia. I mean, why can't we just call it fieldwork? Isn't that what it is, after all? Well, other disciplines do fieldwork as well. What's important here is the cultural in specifically ethnographic fieldwork. Sociologists and others do a lot of fieldwork these days, and some of them even call it "ethnography." But what's missing from most of what they do—what makes it merely fieldwork—is the absence of the cultural.

TR: The distinction between culture and the cultural is really helpful. We're not studying islands of culture. Instead, in my case anyway, we're studying emergent rationalities or technologies. And these are located in concrete venues and there is something meaningful about them, a local aspect that matters, even if that is not the main object of inquiry. The cultural replaces culture.

JF: Yes. And even with this replacement, the anthropologist can remain loyal to the classical Malinowskian project of capturing the imponderabilia of everyday life. This domain of imponderabilia—what remains unthought or subliminal, what is rendered visible and available often through the style or tone of behavior—is one of the domains in which the question of textuality still matters because it was precisely there that Malinowski himself was calling upon the need for narrative and other kinds of informal, non-analytical textualities.

PR: I think this distinction between culture and the cultural is really suggestive. We're not asking for return to a thicker description and are not returning to "key symbols"[2] and the rest. And yet, a diacritic of anthropology is its insistence on the cultural.

GM: I fully agree. In the pursuit of objects, new terrains, we as anthropologists feel we can't, yet, do without culture, but how to make it appear in our analyses, how to make it resonate is a very large problem. Conceptual substitutes for older ideas of culture—based on geographical referents, totalities, holism, tied to forms of life—called for in work in environments of fragmentation and partialities like hybridity don't serve us very well because they were designed for research problems related to identity, the centrality of which I think all of us here think we should be trying to move away from. So we are signaling this as our insistence on preserving the dimension of the cultural, rather than culture, no matter where and how we are moving. I think this still means the cultural as a marker of difference and not as a generic, as in, our common contemporary culture.

PR: Yes, the world has changed. In 1500 in New Guinea, groups may well have been more bounded than they are today, whatever they were like then. And the term certainly gave us a lot of interesting work and taught us a lot about the world, but it seems tied to too many conditions that don't exist any more. The idea that everyone is the same and there are no distinctive differences in meaning and style is ridiculous; there are. But identifying them and explaining them is the challenge.

GM: This was the project of an exceptionally able Korean-American student who wanted to work on the culture of risk among South Korean operators in finance, with the 1997 currency crisis in Asia in mind.[3] While she had advantages for doing fieldwork in Korea on this topic, there were no particular reasons why she should have focused her time and effort there. In fact, if there were ever a subject for a multi-sited design and logic of research, this was it. But there were strong professional and career pressures to make fieldwork local—to look for something, not just situational and historical of the moment, but distinctively cultural—or rather, traditional—about the operations of risk and finance in Korea. Anyhow, she settled into a year of research in venture capital firms. All did not go smoothly in these sites of participant observation, but she returned with rich material, and on the way to her dissertation, she developed really interesting things to say about markets, finance, and the present conditions of modernity as "globalization" and about the ways capital operates through the practices of financial experts. But there was this nagging expectation in producing the dissertation to "make it Korean." What she faced was like the question that you ingeniously dealt with in *French DNA*, the Frenchness within the process, and I recall that several of the reviewers of your book found this very provocative—the idea that DNA, science, can be intimately cultural. But how to achieve this as both insight and effect? This is what our student was facing in producing the dissertation.

PR: Yes. So there are two things we don't want to do. We don't want this Korean-American student to tell us that capitalism is exactly the same everywhere and we don't want this Korean-American student to say that global finance has a uniquely Korean form which is the key to understanding how, say, the Internet and other global things work in Korea.

GM: But in producing the dissertation, these typical pressures are at work. Despite our counter-inclinations, she felt impelled, I presume, to produce an anthropological outcome that meant acknowledging the first injunction you just articulated—don't treat capitalism as if it were the same everywhere—but going against the second. She felt that she had to go after the key to capitalist modernity Korean-style. Venture capital as a local piece of fundamentally global expertise pressures the student who might have been better off not to have spent so much time in Korea to see it as the same—as part of an international culture of enclosed expertise—but also different because it is in Korea. The distinction between culture and the cultural that we are driving at was a key issue here. She didn't yet feel herself able to work confidently with the latter rather than the former concept.

TR: For studying everyday life—say, in relation to Korean shamanism—a kind of Geertzian thick description might work. Then the object of study is culture. However, if one analyzes finance and the way it is practiced, then culture is not the actual object of analysis. In order to be analytically successful, one needs to conceptualize the object of analysis differently—with such heuristically valuable terms as assemblage, apparatus, multi-sitedness, and so forth. They allow us—if I understand you correctly—to arrange "Korean finance" into several heterogeneous elements. One of these elements can be the cultural, which is definitely of relevance to "Korean" finance.

GM: Right.

PR: So, the concept of the cultural allows one to approach or assess the object of analysis better and in a more adequate way than the idea of culture, because culture somehow requires that everything else is subsumed under it.

BUILDING BRIDGES INTO THE NEW

GM: Yes. I like to avoid the notion of culture as such, because it's so intractable—our peculiar burden. Latour really is playing around with anthropology but within the categories of sociology. So he really doesn't have our sense of problem or burden.

TR: Can you say more about how culture is our "peculiar burden"?

GM: It's a habit of classic anthropological thought. It's still apparent in the discourse of many anthropologists. One may play with globalization, but foremost you've got to "understand the culture." Behind it all, there is India, and you can know what India is. It's a very classic view, and it's not gone at all. We don't need to disrupt our thinking in terms of it, but it is an unavoidable burden, especially when we speak to anthropologists who will inevitably ask: "Well, what about culture?" Culture, in some sense of the term, is not supplementary to the discipline but remains distinctive to it. So we have to address this.

PR: Where's the problem? Science is universal, but human beings do it so that means it's historical, and it could have been otherwise, and it's contingent. I'm in France, and she's in Korea. At some level, identifying what's Korean or French about this situation is simple. I mean, if you've seen any French movie, the fact that there's going to be a discourse of seduction that goes on between the genders is not a surprise, and it's certainly very important to them. So we're interested in the interfaces of the science in the French lab with these French actors who were not peasants. So it's more a question of how much you want to push it. Do you want to say what really, really, counts there is the Frenchness? If so, you'd look ridiculous. On the other hand, we know from Latour that a lot of work goes into making science or finance universal and that that work is never complete. So it depends on how you decide on a problem and on significance. But I know that that doesn't satisfy people who want a big answer to the question.

GM: They just need to know what its relation if any is to that other thing—the predictable cinematic seduction scene.

TR: So you are asking Paul to articulate the kind of anthropology he is doing in a friendly, almost didactic way so that people who are concerned with culture and don't actually know what he is working on can follow him and see how, in which sense, it is still anthropological in the way that they understand this term.

GM: Right. There are all sorts of perfectly valid ways to bring the scripts we know and the "markings" of anthropology into these new terrains. Our discussions have made an inventory of them, including this example of the dissertation on Korean venture capitalism that I discussed. Often, working around the tropes of identity and exchange makes a treatment sufficiently anthropological, or playing on the polysemy of a metaphor that arises in the course of fieldwork, usually by inflating its significance. We should appreciate and respect what these venerable moves teach us, on the one hand, and be very suspicious of them, on the other, as exhausting the anthropological interest in a novel domain such as finance, or humanitarianism, or markets, or whatever. Finding new terms or concepts for ourselves in the heart of the material, the stuff of fieldwork, whether they are unfamiliar, uncomfortable, or unaesthetic for us, is the essence, for me, of being anthropological. Being able to do this anew in contemporary circumstances is the challenge for which the research function needs to be redefined or restated, and in which, perhaps ironically, the reassuring use of given scripts, tropes, and techniques—for example, of selecting metaphors to stand for the cultural—can be an obstacle.

PR: So the problem is scripts. We are required to answer these venerable questions, or else it's not anthropology.

GM: Right.

PR: So is this method limited by working with scientists? What if you were working with taxi drivers or people in the slums of Rio? Could you do this kind of work in those settings, or is this crafted for very specific settings? And this is where your idea of scripts comes back? I think that's the blockage, but even if—which may never happen—eventually the scripts wear out and even the people writing them are bored with them, what would come next?

GM: Well, I think you do the old anthropology, or apply the venerable strategies for making it anthropological, where your object is constructed by life as you find it—everyday life. And, indeed, classic fieldwork training teaches you to prepare or invent the scene or site of study to do just this; I recall here an old collection, not read anymore, that argued just this—it was called *Open Minds, Closed Systems*.[4] But we can't afford this anymore, which, I think, is widely understood after *Writing Culture*. Yet, fealty to the method, even in the very changed circumstances in which it is practiced now, still requires considering competing and overlapping zones of representations as existing alongside what is encountered through the privileged direct experience within the scenes of fieldwork, and thus made ethnographic. These other zones of representations—as social facts, Paul once said—must be incorporated by design as scenes of fieldwork as well. We discussed this at various points when we talked of the way that fieldwork emerges starkly in the dissertation project as preparation here to go elsewhere, or "over there," when in fact the relation of here to there now is organic and graduated. The emergence of the reflexive subject as a trope of research makes one sensitive to the idea that there is very little one can think or imagine in the confines of academic study that is not already thought in some version, expression, or venue in sites and scenes of fieldwork. These discursive chains that link one to one's eventual literal subjects of fieldwork must be thought through and addressed analytically in constituting the very notion of fieldwork for each project of research. To do so creates additional beneficial complexity in the formulation of research in anthropology, and makes visible in the places and spaces of fieldwork a lot that has been elided, kept to the margins, or just not seen for the sake of finding traditional subjects within accustomed scripts. To understand the problem in this way gets us beyond the question of "Is the subaltern included?" in our considerations. Again, it is no longer a question of whether the more traditional subjects of anthropology get ignored if we seem to be focusing on elite or expert subjects. Rather the kind of research in which we seem to be interested is no longer simply the ethnography of X and their way of life. The field of research that we have been discussing, and in which we have been primarily interested, emerges in a much different way. We have to do things differently in the professional culture of method.

PR: I agree.

IN THE DESIGN STUDIO

TR: And this is, as both of you have suggested above, where the design studio gains momentum. Perhaps one could describe the idea of a design studio as a major outcome of our conversations, the need for a design studio, understood as a kind of training space in which one could fuse what Jim and George have called epistemology and ontology. Said in other words, the design studio could be a place in which students could be taught—could experience—how to anthropologize all the information that they have assembled on their particular topic before they actually begin fieldwork. Such a practice would render palpable the significance of an anthropological toolkit, so that whatever would happen in fieldwork, the student would be equipped with a certain anthropological sensibility. A second important result of our conversations, or so I think, is what we have called 'mode' or 'mode of research.' In *Athropos Today* there is one chapter about mode. It is about Paul Klee. The point of the chapter is to not read Klee's oeuvre in order to learn about his worldview, "this is how Klee saw nature or geometry or composition," etc. What matters instead is Klee's mode of looking at things, of taking them up, of decomposing them into elements in motion. This mode is what the kind of anthropology of the contemporary we have been discussing is interested in. This Klee-inspired mode is not limited to working with scientific experts, with wealthy people, with migrant workers, with illegal workers. It is applicable to all these domains without being dogmatic because it implies that the researcher always has to keep in mind that what she actually studies exists only in this special arena. In other words, it is always about a specific and distinct singularity, to recognize which is the key move in this mode of analysis.

PR: I think that's an elegant summary. The only thing I would add is that because there are singularities involved, there must be differences in doing this other kind of work. As we enlarge this, we would need to include in the tool kit problems of access, problems of understanding, problems of language; those should remain open. But your idea that it's a sensibility, an ethos, which is not restricted to one sphere, I think that's nicely said.

Tobias Rees

The presentation of knowledge or thoughts in books or scholarly articles is often conclusive, the "finished" result of research, reflection, and analysis. But where is there place for the discussion of the yet tentative, inconclusive? For thought experiments in need of being tested, discussed, reworked, or refuted? If one takes the view that knowledge formation is a process, then it seems important to find a form adequate to that process, in which the fluidity and tentativeness of things predominate. The taped and transcribed (and reworked) presentation of a lively scholarly exchange on contested topics appears to be one form of taking up the challenge of presenting thinking in motion.

In the conversations across generations presented here, George Marcus and Paul Rabinow explore some of the ways in which anthropology has been developing since the 1980s and seek to articulate, in a constantly challenging back-and-forth, the conceptual challenges these developments imply for the practice of anthropological inquiry today. Today, what is anthropology? What could it be? Where does it come from and in which ways might it develop? What's the role of culture, the place of society, where we anthropologists no longer exclusively—or predominantly—address culture and/or society? What new objects have been emerging? What new concepts? What's the role of fieldwork under these renewed circumstances? What constitutes ethnographic data and what could serve as a measure for descriptive thickness?

To rehearse the different answers tried out as possible responses to these questions would run counter to the open-ended and querulous quality of our exchanges. In this afterword, therefore, one will neither find a glossary of the concepts we have developed in passing (e.g., the contemporary, the untimely, the adjacent, the cultural, the paraethnographic, etc.) nor a synthetic summary of the ways in which these concepts may help to establish points of connection between what I might call the traditional anthropological and research in terrains classically believed to be outside anthropological expertise (e.g., science, finance, media, law, etc.). Instead, the following pages offer a brief sketch of what is arguably the central idea (vision?) developed in the course of the conversation, and of how both Rabinow and Marcus have taken it up and developed it further, namely the idea of "design" and "design studio."

The term "design" refers to both the form fieldwork/inquiry takes and the form of textual presentation to which it might lead. More specifically, it expresses the pedagogical effort to teach students the art of finding the design of research—and of its eventual textualization—in the course of inquiry, to let the field or the particular story or theme that is emerging take over the design. The challenge is to become part of a foreign milieu, to submit to the outside, to get drowned in and carried away by it, while staying alert to the gradual emergence of a theme to which chance encounters, fugitive events, anecdotal observations give rise. In short, the term design emphasizes the significance of long-term research, the need to be sensitive to the singularity of the field site, and the art of not letting one's research and thinking be dominated by well-established theories and/or tacit norms of what fieldwork "is," of what a published monograph should look like (in the conversation we speak of "scripts"). As such, the term design expresses the primacy of inquiry and data over theory, which all four of us affirm as an essential feature of anthropological knowledge production.

The "design studio"—a phrase developed with the architectural design studio or lab meetings in the sciences in mind—is the institutional space for teaching an anthropology informed by the design concept as sketched above. It could be described as a platform for fusing research and teaching—as place for teaching the basic equipment of anthropological concepts and techniques; for presenting first research reports (by professors as well as students); for becoming familiar with relevant literature; for becoming sensitive to the always unique and singular story emerging in the course of fieldwork; for discussing what constitutes data; etc. The aim is to fuse research, pedagogy, and ongoing concept-work in order to push anthropological research in new (but disciplinarily coherent) directions, in order to move beyond established scripts and to learn something new (but without leaving disciplinary norms and forms behind). Furthermore, the design studio teaches science as analytical and ethical practice.

Since the time of our conversations, April 2004, both Marcus and Rabinow have taken up the idea of a design studio, have refined and institutionalized it.

CENTER FOR ETHNOGRAPHY, UNIVERSITY OF CALIFORNIA, IRVINE

In 2005, Marcus left the Department of Anthropology at Rice University and became a professor at the University of California, Irvine. Once at Irvine, Marcus began to institutionalize the Center for Ethnography: http://www.socsci.uci.edu/~ethnog/. Established in 2006, the Center functions as a platform for theoretical and methodological conversations about ethnographic research practices across disciplines today. It is explicitly devoted to documenting and analyzing the transformative effect that work in new terrains has on ethnographic research methodologies and theoretical developments. To that end, it organizes conferences and workshops and invites scholars and students who are exploring new ways of practicing fieldwork.

Specifically, the focus of the Center is on the paraethnographic, which is—I am picking up a recurring theme of the dialogues—Marcus's effort to bring the "epistemological" and the "ontological" together. The attempt is to make conceptually available the shifts that the fieldwork encounter, the data-producing relationship, have undergone since anthropologists entered new terrains of research, such as science, technology, law, media, finance, etc. The effort is to reflect explicitly—with students who already have conducted or are about to begin research—on encounters and engagements with counterpart others who are, almost like the anthropologist/ethnographer, concerned with problems of the emergent, of knowledge production, of institution-building, of strategic decision-making, etc. Furthermore, the Center offers the opportunity (to students as well as to professors) to organize workshops that bring together anthropologists and counterpart others in order to reflect explicitly on collaborations, on shared imaginaries, on difference, and to make these reflections part of research designs.

The rethinking of data-producing relationships in the field, so Marcus hopes, may make available for thought, critique, and innovation the conceptual remaking of the more classic "scenes of encounter" in the field. And this might be of major help in teaching what it means to conduct ethnographic fieldwork today. What sorts of relationships generate data now? What are the forms of data now? What are the bounds of ethnography and fieldwork in such projects located at sites of reflexive knowledge-making? What becomes of critique? What distinctive forms of writing, reporting, and concepts might such projects generate?

The Center for Ethnography, then, might be described as a space for presenting, discussing, and analyzing innovative ethnographic research as well as research on the theoretical and methodological re-functioning of ethnography for contemporary cultural, social, and technological transformations—with the explicit goal of furthering such new practices. In short, the Center might be described as a variant of the design studio idea as developed in the course of our conversation.

ANTHROPOLOGY OF THE CONTEMPORARY RESEARCH COLLABORATORY (ARC), BERKELEY

At the time Rabinow and I went to Rice, in April 2004, we had been discussing the possibility of establishing an Institute for the Anthropology of the Contemporary for more than two years. In 2001/2—when Rabinow was Blaise Pascal Professor in the Department of Philosophy at the École Normale Supérieure (Paris) and I worked as his assistant and prepared my fieldwork—I suggested that he should start a research institute devoted to the anthropological study of the contemporary. Such an institute, I imagined, would be the platform for fieldwork-based philosophical inquiry into emergent phenomena past and present; would seek to trace the changes anthropology has undergone since the 1980s; and would map and seek to address the conceptual and methodological challenges it faces today. For a year we discussed the suggestion and gradually—if hypothetically—what was at first perhaps a naïve idea began to gain contours. The initial vision was to create an institute that would (1) bring together a core group of researchers—mostly but not exclusively anthropologists—around particular projects on phenomena that significantly shape the contemporary, and (2) to use such a research institute as a platform for teaching and reflection on the recent history of anthropology.

In late 2003—due to a generous grant from the Molecular Sciences Institute at Berkeley, a National Center of Excellence for Genomic Sciences— the research institute we had envisioned became a reality and gained its first concrete contours. In a way, the meeting with Marcus and Faubion at Rice was the first official project of the Institute, a means of testing our ideas, involving others, and discussing contemporary anthropology.

In the course of 2004, after we returned from Rice, work on making the center a functioning research institute accelerated. Rabinow, together with a group of past and present students, took the project a significant step further and worked out how organizationally and financially a Research Center for the Anthropology of the Contemporary might look. The decisive step was eventually taken by Rabinow, Stephen Collier (New School), and Andrew Lakoff (U.C. San Diego). Together, they designed the institute as the Anthropology of the Contemporary Research Collaboratory (ARC) and organized it around research projects on (1) the emergent biosecurity apparatus in the U.S. and (2) the ontological remaking of things in the context of synthetic biology and nanotechnology: http://anthropos-lab.net/. Since spring 2005, ARC has functioned as a research collaboratory, has institutionalized blogs, and has produced its own series of working papers: http://anthropos-lab.net/documents. At its core, which is inseparably related to the research project, is a focus on concept-work—anthropological work focused on conceptual motion, and the need to coin concepts adequate to such a focus.

From the time of its inception forward, ARC has been functioning as a platform for graduate training. Rabinow has conducted several "labinars," a term that captures the fusion of a laboratory report on ongoing research and the seminar as a more traditionally established pedagogical form in academia. Students are encouraged to bring their research to the labinar. They are integrated, if loosely, into the research project of the core group and encouraged to connect their own work—in the labinar but as well in the form of blogs and email exchanges—to the ongoing concept-work. In short, the ARC has become a multi-layered design studio, in which research, concept-work, and teaching are closely and inseparably intertwined.

TOWARD A MULTITUDE OF DESIGN STUDIOS

The Center for Ethnography and the Anthropology of the Contemporary Research Collaboratory are but two responses to the open—and exciting— situation in which anthropology finds itself today. Our conversations across generations present one way—one among several others possible— of articulating the challenge inherent in this openness. Others would have offered a different story and would have come up with a different diagnosis and different kinds of possibilities and visions. Indeed, in recent years several—in part divergent, in part complementary—explorations of contemporary anthropology have been published. Each one of them might, at least to some degree, be described as a kind of design studio. In particular—to name but a few—one thinks of the problematization of such classical concepts as the "field" and "culture" by Akhil Gupta and James Ferguson;[1] the problematization of the sacred bundle, the four-field holism of American Anthropology and its discontents, by Sylvia Yanagisako and Daniel Segal;[2] the call for a Neo-Boasian anthropology by

Matti Bunzl, which is explicitly a response to the change and diversification anthropology has undergone since the 1970s;[3] or Michael Fischer's "anthropology outside the frame," which seeks to explore the conditions and possibilities of anthropology at a time when it turns equally to science and to ritual, to the close as well as to the far-away.[4]

The diversity of these approaches, just like the diversity of voices in the dialogues presented here, is a mirror of contemporary anthropology's healthy diversity; an expression of the vitality of a discipline that has been constantly engaged in its own polyphonic process of self-investigation and future charting.

NOTES

INTRODUCTION

1 James Clifford and George E. Marcus, eds., *Writing Culture: The Poetics and Politics of Ethnography* (Berkeley: University of California Press, 1986).

2 One example of this is *Reinventing Anthropology*, ed. Dell Hymes (New York: Pantheon, 1972).

3 Clifford Geertz, *The Interpretation of Cultures* (New York: Basic Books, 1973).

4 Geertz's textual and philological reconceptualization of the culture concept was of wide-ranging significance and influence. On the one hand, it established a large corpus of philosophical writings on the methodologies used in the humanities, particularly philology and cultural history, as immediately relevant to the work of ethnography (I think in particular of a series of German authors, ranging from Ernst Cassirer and Wilhelm Dilthey to Hans-Georg Gadamer and Max Weber). On the other hand, it made ethnography relevant to the humanities, specifically to cultural history. For a review of Geertz's significance for cultural history, see chapter 3 of Peter Burke's *What is Cultural History?* (Cambridge: Polity Press, 2004).

5 Cf. especially Michel Foucault, *Power/Knowledge: Selected Interviews and Other Writings, 1972–1977*, ed. Colin Gordon (New York: Pantheon, 1980).

6 Michael J. Fischer and George E. Marcus, *Anthropology as Cultural Critique: An Experimental Moment in the Human Sciences* (Chicago: University of Chicago Press, 1986).

7 Paul Rabinow, *Anthropos Today. Reflections on Modern Equipment* (Princeton: Princeton University Press, 2003), 84.

8 Paul Rabinow, *Making PCR: A Story of Biotechnology* (Princeton: Princeton University Press, 1996); *French DNA: Trouble in Purgatory* (Princeton: Princeton University Press, 1999); and with Talia Dan-Cohen, *A Machine to Make a Future: Biotech Chronicles* (Princeton: Princeton University Press, 2004).

9 Rabinow's anthropology of reason has several installations, beginning as such with *French Modern: Norms and Forms of the Social Environment* (Cambridge: MIT Press, 1989; Chicago: University of Chicago Press, 1995). It is followed by the trilogy noted above, *Anthropos Today* and *Essays in the Anthropology of Reason* (Princeton: Princeton University Press, 1996).

10 Marcus has consistently published scholarly articles on the transformation of ethnography. Cf. most notably his collected *Ethnography Through Thick and Thin* (Princeton: Princeton University Press, 1998).

11 The need for and specification of alternative anthropological pedagogies are the central themes of Marcus and Faubion's *Fieldwork Is Not What It Used to Be: Anthropology's Culture of Method in Transition* (forthcoming 2009).

DIALOGUE I   ANTHROPOLOGY IN MOTION

1 Clifford Geertz (d. 2006) was at the forefront of American cultural anthropology from the later 1960s to the early 1980s. His most important works include *The Religion of Java* (Glencoe, Ill.: The Free Press, 1960), *Islam Observed: Religious Development in Morocco and Indonesia* (New Haven: Yale University Press, 1968); *Negara: The Theater-state in Nineteenth-century Bali* (Princeton: Princeton University Press, 1980), and two collections of essays: *The Interpretation of Cultures*, cited in the Introduction, and *Local Knowledge: Further Essays in Interpretive Anthropology* (New York: Basic Books, 1983).

2 During the 1950s, the Ford Foundation provided some $270 million in training and research fellowships to American universities to strengthen American knowledge of and the capacity for service in Africa, Asia, the Middle East, and Latin America. Such major research universities as Harvard and MIT were beneficiaries of Ford Foundation funding, which stimulated the development of ambitious collaborative programs. The Harvard Department of Social Relations was exemplary of the trend. Under the guidance of social theorist Talcott Parsons (1902–1979), the Harvard program pursued the synthesis of the ideas of such classical social theorists as Emile Durkheim (1858–1917) and Max Weber (1864–1920), the latter the founder of interpretive sociology and a significant influence on Geertz's practice of anthropology.

3 In the post-war period, MIT won national prominence as a center of the design of sophisticated new technological systems, many of which were di-

rected toward contributing to the solution to such problems of the developing world as malnutrition and epidemic disease.

4   Marcus alludes to Bronislaw Malinowski (1884–1942) and Franz Boas (1858–1942). Trained at the London School of Economics, Malinowski was among the leaders in transforming anthropological research from an armchair enterprise to one involving the extended observation of the everyday life of the subjects under study. His venerable outline of ethnographic method appears as the introduction of his *Argonauts of the Western Pacific* (New York: E. P. Dutton & Co., 1922). Franz Boas is the founder of American cultural anthropology. Like Malinowski, he insisted on the anthropologist's extended and intimate engagement with the people of his or her study. Unlike Malinowski, Boas conceived of anthropology as a mode of historical inquiry directed first and foremost toward the particularity of cultural formations rather than toward the extrapolation of cultural universals.

5   The Golden Age of American anthropology is dominated by such students of Boas as Ruth Benedict (1887–1948), Alfred Kroeber (1876–1960), and Margaret Mead (1901–1978). It is a period not simply of the expansion of the discipline's professional ranks and departmental centers, but also of relatively cordial and collaborative relations between anthropologists and the U.S. government. Those relations sour considerably with the expansion of the Vietnam conflict in the 1960s, and the Golden Age deteriorates with them.

6   At the invitation of its founders, sociologist Edward Shils (1911–1985) and political scientist David Apter, Geertz joined the Committee for the Comparative Study of New Nations at the University of Chicago in 1962. Devoted to the study of processes of state-formation in postcolonial Africa, Asia, and Latin America, the committee was an interdisciplinary venture among economists, sociologists, political scientists, and anthropologists.

7   Bellah was trained at and then taught at Harvard University. He first became acquainted with Clifford Geertz in the late 1950s when he was a professor and Geertz a student in Parsons' Department of Social Relations.

8   See Cohn, *Colonialism and Its Forms of Knowledge: The British in India* (Princeton: Princeton University Press, 1996).

9   The phrase alludes to a volume that Parsons co-edited with Edward Shils, *Toward a General Theory of Action* (New York: Harper & Row, 1951).

10 Geertz joined the faculty of the Institute in 1970. Three years later, he would occupy the first chair of the newly inaugurated School of Social Science at the Institute, a post he would continue to occupy until his retirement in 2000.

11 The subjects of Malinowski's *Argonauts of the Western Pacific*.

12 Once the protégé of Talcott Parsons, social theorist Niklas Luhmann (1927–1999) is the chief architect of that fusion of sociological functionalism and cybernetics known as systems theory.

13 Anthropologist Victor Turner (1920–1983) was trained at the University of Manchester and worked extensively in Africa, where he developed the analysis of the deployment of symbols in action that came to be known as symbolic anthropology. He came to the University of Chicago in 1968.

14 Marshall Sahlins (b. 1930) came to Chicago in 1973 in the aftermath of spending several years in Paris, where he came into contact with Claude Lévi-Strauss and Lévi-Strauss's structuralism. His later career has been devoted to the analysis of the differential impact of historical events on collective systems of meaning and the broader enterprise of a historical anthropology.

15 John and Jean Comaroff are scholars of colonial and postcolonial South Africa; they are also distinguished contributors to historical anthropology. See their *Of Revelation and Revolution*, Volume 1: Christianity, Colonialism and Consciousness in South Africa (Chicago: University of Chicago Press, 1991).

16 Paul Rabinow, *Reflections on Fieldwork in Morocco* (Berkeley: University of California Press, 1977).

17 Thomas Kuhn develops his idea of paradigms and their exhaustion in his influential *Structure of Scientific Revolutions* (Chicago: University of Chicago Press, 1962).

18 Robert Maynard Hutchins (1899–1977) served as the president and chancellor of the University of Chicago between 1929 and 1951. He was a champion of the teaching of the Western canon and of the breadth and seriousness of liberal education.

19 See Geertz, "Thick Description: Toward an Interpretive Theory of Culture," the opening chapter of his *The Interpretation of Cultures*.

20 David Schneider, a professor in the Department of Anthropology at the University of Chicago at the time, was an outspoken critic of the Vietnam War.

21 Arjun Appadurai is an anthropological theorist of the postcolonial and global cultural economy.

22 Nicholas Dirks is an anthropological historian of colonialism.

23 Protégé of Leo Strauss, Allan Bloom is the author of *The Closing of the American Mind* (New York: Simon & Schuster, 1987).

24 See Marcus's *The Nobility and the Chiefly Tradition in the Modern Kingdom of Tonga* (Wellington: The Polynesia Society, 1980).

25 With Dick Cushman, Marcus wrote "Ethnographies as Texts," *Annual Review of Anthropology* 11 (1982):25–69.

26 Clifford, *Person and Myth: Maurice Leenhardt in the Melanesian World* (Berkeley: University of California Press, 1981). French anthropologist Maurice Leenhardt (1878–1954) was a specialist in the Kanak people of New Caledonia.

27 Gerald Berreman, a specialist in South Asia and social stratification, was a contributor to *Rethinking Anthropology.*

28 Alexander Woodside is currently Professor of Chinese and Southeast Asian History at the University of British Columbia.

29 Specialist in pre- and post-war Vietnam, David G. Marr is the author of *Vietnamese Anticolonialism, 1885–1925* (Berkeley: University of California Press, 1971) and *Vietnam 1945: The Quest for Power* (Berkeley: University of California Press, 1995).

30 See, e.g., Elenore Smith Bowen (pseudonym of Laura Bohannon), *Return to Laughter* (Garden City, N.Y.: Doubleday, 1964); Claude Lévi-Strauss, *Tristes Tropiques*, trans. John and Doreen Weightman (New York: Atheneum, 1974 [originally published in 1955]).

31 Marxist anthropologist Eric Wolf (1923–1999) specialized in Latin America and is author of *Europe and the People without History* (Berkeley: University of California Press).

32 Anthropologist and sociologist Pierre Bourdieu (1930–2002) assumed the chair in sociology at the Collège de France in 1981; he was also director of the Centre de Sociologie Européenne from 1968 until his death.

33 Sahlins, *Waiting for Foucault, Still* (Chicago: Prickly Paradigm Press, 2002).

34 The critique appears in "I-witnessing: Malinowski's Children," in Geertz's *Works and Lives: The Anthropologist as Author* (Stanford: Stanford University Press, 1988), pp. 73–101.

35 Laura Nader, a professor of anthropology at the University of California, Berkeley, was one of the contributors to Hymes's *Reinventing Anthropology.*

36 Eleanor Leacock (1922–1987) served as chair of the department of anthropology at The City University of New York from 1972 until her death. She was a leading Marxist ethnohistorian.

37 Sherry Ortner remains a leading feminist anthropologist. A recent collection of her essays has appeared under the title *Anthropology and Social Theory: Culture, Power, and the Acting Subject* (Durham: Duke University Press, 2006).

38 The site of the conference that led to the publication of *Writing Culture* took place at the School for American Research, located in Santa Fe, New Mexico.

39 Marvin Harris (1927–2001) was a leading anthropological practitioner of the materialist and functionalist analysis of cultural beliefs and practices.

40 Robert Paul is the author of *Tibetan Symbolic Worlds: Psychoanalytic Explorations* (Chicago: University of Chicago Press, 1982).

41 "Toward a Reflexive and Critical Anthropology," in *Reinventing Anthropology*, ed. Dell Hymes (New York: Pantheon, 1972).

42 See Johannes Fabian, "Language, History, and Anthropology," *Journal for the Philosophy of the Social Sciences* 1:1: 1971. Fabian graduated with a Ph.D. in anthropology from the University of Chicago in 1969.

43 See *First-Time: The Historical Vision of an Afro-American People*, 2nd ed. (Chicago: University of Chicago Press, 2002 [originally published in 1983]).

44 See *Ilongot Headhunting, 1883–1974* (Stanford: Stanford University Press, 1980).

45 *Time and the Other: How Anthropology Makes Its Object* (New York: Columbia University Press, 1983).

46 Landmark feminist works of the period include several important collections. See among others *Gender and Kinship: Essays toward a Unified Analysis*, ed. Jane Fishburne Collier and Sylvia Junko Yanagisako (Stanford: Stanford University Press, 1987); *Nature, Culture, and Gender*, ed. Carol P. MacCormack and Marilyn Strathern (Cambridge: Cambridge University Press, 1980); *Sexual Meanings: The Cultural Construction of Gender and Sexuality*, ed. Sherry Ortner and Harriet Whitehead (Cambridge: Cambridge University Press, 1981); *Toward an Anthropology of Women*, ed. Rayna Rapp Reiter (New York: Monthly Review Press, 1975); and *Women, Culture, and Society*, ed. Michelle Rosaldo and Louise Lamphere (Stanford: Stanford University Press, 1974). The best known feminist response to *Writing Culture* is another collection: *Women Writing Culture*, ed. Ruth Behar and Deborah A. Gordon (Berkeley: University of California Press, 1995).

47 Former Director of the Wenner-Gren Foundation for Anthropological Research, one of the major sources of funding for research in the discipline, Sydel Silverman is Professor Emerita at the CUNY Graduate Center.

DIALOGUE II   AFTER *WRITING CULTURE*

1 See Barth's introduction in *Ethnic Groups and Boundaries. The Social Organization of Culture Difference* ed. Frederik Barth (Oslo: Universitetsforlaget, 1969).

2 The Public Culture project coalesced in the mid-1980s among a group of scholars inclined to accept social theorist Jürgen Habermas's diagnosis that the emergence of such social movements as feminism and environmentalism signaled the resurgence of publics bound together by common values and united against the technocratic management of social policy.

3 Many of the participants in the Public Culture project—Arjun Appadurai, Carol Breckenridge, Benjamin Lee, Dilip Gaonkar, Lauren Berlant, Michael

Warner, and Craig Calhoun—were or are connected to the Chicago-based Center for Transcultural Studies (previously known as the Center for Psychosocial Studies). The founding director was University of Chicago–trained Lee.

4   See William Mazzarella, *Shoveling Smoke: Advertising and Globalization in Contemporary India* (Durham: Duke University Press, 2003).

5   See Arjun Appadurai, ed., *The Social Life of Things: Commodities in Cultural Perspective* (New York: Cambridge University Press, 1986).

6   Daniel Miller is currently Professor of Material Culture in the department of anthropology at University College London. Among his relevant publications are an edited collection, *Material Culture: Why Some Things Matter* (London: UCL Press, 1998), and *The Dialectics of Shopping* (Chicago: University of Chicago Press, 2001).

7   See James D. Faubion, *Modern Greek Lessons: A Primer in Historical Constructivism* (Princeton: Princeton University Press, 1993).

8   Bruno Latour is Professor at the Institut d'Etudes Politiques de Paris and a leading figure in science and technology studies. Relevant works include his *Science in Action: How to Follow Scientists and Engineers through Society* (Cambridge, Mass.: Harvard University Press, 1987) and *Reassembling the Social: An Introduction to Actor-network Theory* (Oxford: Oxford University Press, 2005).

9   Rees alludes here to Hans-Jörg Rheinberger's *Toward a History of Epistemic Things: Synthesizing Protein in the Test Tube* (Stanford: Stanford University Press, 1997).

10 See *Biographies of Scientific Objects* (Chicago: University of Chicago Press, 2000) and Daston's edited volume, *Things that Talk: Object Lessons from Art and Science* (Cambridge, Mass.: MIT Press, 2004).

11 The list of such work is long. See, for example, Sarah Franklin and Helen Ragoné, eds., *Reproducing Reproduction: Kinship, Power, and Technological Innovation* (Philadelphia: University of Pennsylvania Press, 1998); Heather Paxson, *Making Modern Mothers: Ethics and Family Planning in Urban Greece* (Berkeley: University of California Press, 2004); Rayna Rapp, *Testing Women, Testing the Fetus: The Social Impact of Amniocentesis in America* (New York: Routledge, 1999); and Charis Thompson, *Making Parents: The Ontological Choreography of Reproductive Technologies* (Cambridge, Mass.: MIT Press, 2005).

12 See Strathern, *After Nature: English Kinship in the Late Twentieth Century* (Cambridge: Cambridge University Press, 1992) and *Reproducing the Future: Essays on Anthropology, Kinship, and the New Reproductive Technologies* (New York: Routledge, 1992).

13 See Caitlin Zaloom, *Out of the Pits: Trading and Technology from Chicago to London* (Chicago: University of Chicago Press, 2006).

14 See, among others, Marc Abélès, *The Politics of Survival* (Duke University Press translation forthcoming); David Kennedy, *The Dark Side of Humanitarianism: Reassessing International Humanitarianism* (Princeton: Princeton University Press, 2004); and Peter Nyers, *Rethinking Refugees: Beyond States of Emergency* (New York: Routledge, 2006).

15 See Horace Miner's parodic treatment of American customs, "Body Ritual among the Nacirema," *American Anthropologist* 58 (1956): 503–7.

16 See, for example, Marilyn Strathern, *Partial Connections* (Savage, Md.: Rowman & Littlefield, 1991).

DIALOGUE III ANTHROPOLOGY TODAY

1 See the 1983 interview with Rabinow and Hurbert Dreyfus, "On the Genealogy of Ethics: Overview of Work in Progress," in Paul Rabinow, ed., *Essential Works of Michel Foucualt*, vol. 1, *Ethics* (New York: The New Press, 1997), p. 256.

2 See Douglas R. Holmes and George E. Marcus, "Cultures of Expertise and the Management of Globalization: Toward the Re-functioning of Ethnography," in Aiwha Ong and Stephen J. Collier, eds., *Global Assemblages: Technology, Politics, and Ethics as Anthropological Problems* (Malden, Mass.: Blackwell, 2005).

3 These terms are an important part of the conceptual ensemble that Rabinow sets out in *Anthropos Today*. They provide much of the analytical apparatus of the trilogy of Rabinow's recent investigative monographs—*Making PCR, French DNA*, and *A Machine to Make a Future*—to which Marcus alludes here.

4 Anthropologist Stanley Diamond (1922–1991) was the author of several books of poetry, including *Totems* (Barrytown, N.Y.: Open Book Publishers, 1982).

5 The famous phrase appears in Malinowski's *Argonauts of the Western Pacific*. Geertz appropriates the phrase in his 'From the Native's Point of View': On the Nature of Anthropological Understanding, in *Local Knowledge: Further Essays in Interpretive Anthropology* (New York: Basic Books, 1980).

6 See Hans Blumenberg, *The Legitimacy of the Modern Age*, trans. Robert M. Wallace (Cambridge, Mass.: MIT Press, 1983).

7 See Vered Amit, ed., *Constructing the Field: Ethnographic Fieldwork in the Contemporary World* (New York: Routledge, 2000).

1   Rabinow alludes to Luhmann's discussion of the "politics of understanding" in the fourth chapter of his *Observations on Modernity* (Stanford: Stanford University Press, 1998), pp. 69–70.

2   The topic of temporality in anthropology is the central theme of Rabinow's *Marking Time: On the Anthropology of the Contemporary* (Princeton: Princeton University Press, 2007).

3   Rabinow, *Symbolic Domination: Cultural Form and Historical Change in Morocco* (Chicago: University of Chicago Press, 1975), p. 1.

4   The German term is often translated as "science," though its semantic range is much broader than the English suggests. As an enterprise grounded in critical reflection, its pursuit requires a certain remove from the immediacy of any historical moment.

5   The German term, similar to the Greek *paideia*, denotes not merely formal education but a broader experiential and ethical cultivation of the self.

6   In *The Genealogy of Morals* and elsewhere, Friedrich Nietzsche (1844–1900) treats ressentiment, or the erosive emotional goad of the repressed experience of insults and debasement, as the inspiration for the ascetic and anti-aristocratic "slave revolt in morals."

7   The Anthropology of the Contemporary Research Collaboratory (ARC), www.anthropos-lab.net, is an enterprise devoted to collaborative research, pedagogy, and concept work. See the afterword of the present volume.

8   The labor of scientific investigation: see *Anthropos Today*, pp. 83–90.

9   Beyond Holmes's and Marcus's "The Culture of Expertise," see especially the third and fourth chapters of Marcus's *Ethnography through Thick and Thin*.

10   Rabinow's critique, entitled "The Legitimacy of the Contemporary," appears in *Marking Time* (Princeton: Princeton University Press, 2007).

11   Marcus reflects on the ethnographer's complicity with his or her subjects in a 1997 essay entitled "The Uses of Complicity in the Changing Mise-en-scène of Fieldwork," *Representations* 59 (1997): 85–108. He first develops the concept of multi-sited fieldwork in "Anthropology in/of the World System," *Annual Review of Anthropology* 24 (1995): 95–117, reprinted in *Ethnography through Thick and Thin*. On paraethnography, see Holmes's and Marcus's "Cultures of Expertise and the Management of Globalization: Toward the Re-Functioning of Ethnography," in *Global Assemblages*.

12   On imaginaries, see especially Marcus's introduction to *Ethnography through Thick and Thin*.

1 Technicians of general ideas figure prominently first in Rabinow's *French Modern*.

2 See the fourth chapter of Rabinow's *Anthropos Today*.

3 See Marcus, "Imagining the Whole: Ethnography's Contemporary Efforts to Situate Itself," *Critique of Anthropology* 9.3 (1990): 7–30. Originally published in 1989, it appears as the first chapter of *Ethnography through Thick and Thin*.

4 Philosopher Gilbert Ryle's notion of "thick" or contextually sensitive description comes into anthropology through Geertz's introduction of it in "Thick Description: Toward an Interpretive Theory of Culture," the first chapter of *The Interpretation of Cultures*.

5 See especially pp. 18–19 of *Ethnography through Thick and Thin*.

6 See Marcus's more elaborate reflections on the belated temporality of ethnographic research and textualization, "On the Unbearable Slowness of Being an Anthropologist Now: Notes on a Contemporary Anxiety in the Making of Ethnography," *XCP: Cross-Cultural Poetics* 12 (2003): 7–20.

7 Adrian Petryna's *Life Exposed: Biological Citizenship after Chernobyl* (Princeton: Princeton University Press, 2002), and Kim Fortun's *Advocacy after Bhopal: Environmentalism, Disaster, New Global Orders* (Chicago: University of Chicago Press, 2001) were joint winners of the 2003 Sharon Stephens First Book Award of the American Ethnological Society.

8 Gregory Bateson, *Naven: A Survey of the Problems Suggested by a Composite Picture of the Culture of a New Guinea Tribe Drawn from Three Points of View* (Cambridge, Eng.: The University Press, 1936).

9 See "Polemics, Politics, and Problematizations," in *Essential Works of Michel Foucault*, vol. 1, *Ethics*, p. 114.

DIALOGUE VI   OF TIMING AND TEXTS

1 Raymond Williams was a leading figure in the Birmingham School of Cultural Studies. See among other works his *Marxism and Literature* (Oxford: Oxford University Press, 1977).

2 The particular allusion here is to *The Shadows and Lights of Waco: Millennialism Today* (Princeton: Princeton University Press, 2001).

3 One of the eminent American novelists of paranoia, Pynchon is the author of, among other things, *V., A Novel* (Philadelphia: Lippincott, 1963), *The Crying*

of Lot 49 (Philadelphia: Lippincott, 1966), and *Gravity's Rainbow* (New York: Viking Press, 1973).

4 Jamer Hunt has recently accepted a position at the Parsons School of Design, New School University.

5 Michael Taussig, *The Nervous System* (New York: Routledge, 1992).

6 Salvador Dalí, *Conquest of the Irrational*, trans. David Gascoyne (New York: Julien Levy, 1935).

7 Rem Koolhaas's *Delirious New York: A Retroactive Manifesto for Manhattan* (New York: Oxford University Press, 1998).

8 See Dialogue V.

9 Paul Willis, *Learning to Labour: How Working-class Kids Get Working-class Jobs* (New York: Columbia University Press, 1977); see also Marcus's commentary on Willis, "Contemporary Problems of Ethnography in the Modern World System," in *Writing Culture*.

10 Anna Lowenhaupt Tsing is the author of *In the Realm of the Diamond Queen* (Princeton: Princeton University Press, 1993) and *Friction: An Ethnography of Global Connection* (Princeton: Princeton University Press, 2005).

11 See Rabinow, *Anthropos Today*, pp. 131–33.

DIALOGUE VII DESIGNS

1 The distinction is hardly original to this discussion. Lila Abu-Lughod, for example, makes much of it in "Writing Against Culture," her contribution to *Recapturing Capturing Anthropology: Working in the Present*, ed. Richard G. Fox (Santa Fe: School of American Research, 1991).

2 Geertz develops the notion of the key symbol in "Ethos, World View, and the Analysis of Sacred Symbols," the fifth chapter of *The Interpretation of Cultures*.

3 Jae Chung, *The Cultural Tempo of Korean Modernity: Celerity in Venture Industry* (Ph.D. diss., Rice University, Department of Anthropology, 2003).

4 The collection, edited by Max Gluckman, bears the title *Closed Systems and Open Minds: The Limits of Naïvety in Anthropology* (London: Aldine Publishing Company, 1964).

AFTERWORD

Notes

1 Akhil Gupta and James Ferguson, *Anthropological Locations: Boundaries and Grounds of a Field Science* (Berkeley: University of California Press, 1997);

Akhil Gupta and James Ferguson, *Culture, Power, Place: Explorations in Critical Anthropology* (Durham: Duke University Press, 1997). For another recent problematization see the volume edited by Robin Fox and Barbara King, *Anthropology Beyond Culture* (Oxford and New York: Berg Publishers, 2002).

2 Daniel Segal and Sylvia Yanagisako, *Unwrapping the Sacred Bundle: Reflections on the Disciplining of Anthropology* (Durham: Duke University Press, 2005).

3 Matti Bunzl, "Boas, Foucault, and the 'Native Anthropologist': Notes toward a Neo-Boasian Anthropology," *American Anthropologist* 106:3 (2003): 435–42.

4 Michael J. Fischer, *Emergent Forms of Life and the Anthropology of Voice* (Durham: Duke University Press, 2003).

INDEX

actor-network theory, 107. *See also* Latour, Bruno

Advocacy after Bhopal (Fortun), 87–89, 132 n. 7

Althusser, Louis, 4, 18, 27

American Anthropologist, 37, 47

American Ethnologist, 37, 47

Amit, Vered, 53

Anthropology of the Contemporary Research Collaboratory (University of California, Berkeley), 119–20, 131 n. 7

Anthropos Today (Rabinow), 6, 8, 41–42, 48, 101, 113, 124 n. 9, 130 n. 3, 131 n. 8, 132 n. 2 (dialogue v), 133 n. 11

Appadurai, Arjun, 19, 37–38, 126 n. 21, 128 n. 3

"apparatus," 6, 49, 70, 75, 92, 99, 109, 130 n. 3

area studies, 14, 31, 37

Arendt, Hannah, 19–20

Aristotle, 19–20

Aron, Raymond, 19

art, 47

"assemblage," 6, 49, 58, 70, 75, 77, 79, 92–94, 99, 109, 130 n. 3

authority, 7, 38–39, 61, 84–85, 96, 105

Balandier, Georges, 23

Barth, Fredrik, 34

Barthes, Roland, 4

Bateson, Gregory, 35, 88

Bell, Daniel, 21

Bellah, Robert, 15, 125 n. 7

Benedict, Ruth, 35, 125 n. 5

Berreman, Gerald, 23, 26, 127 n. 27

Bildung, 18, 65, 131 n. 5. *See also* pedagogy

Biographies of Scientific Objects (Daston), 39

Bloom, Allan, 20, 126 n. 23

Blumenberg, Hans, 51

Boas, Franz, 2, 14, 125 nn. 4–5; Neo-Boasian anthropology, 120–21

Bourdieu, Pierre, 26, 127 n. 32

Buddenbrooks (Mann), 42
Bunzl, Matti, 121

Cambridge University, 17, 20
capitalism, 27, 36, 41–42, 90, 96, 98, 108–9. *See also* finance
Cassirer, Ernst, 4, 123 n. 4
Cavell, Stanley, 21
Celera Diagnostics, 50, 76–77, 90–91. See also *Machine to Make a Future*
Center for Ethnography (University of California, Irvine), 117–18
City University of New York (CUNY), 27, 127 n. 36, 128 n. 47
Clifford, James, 21, 27
Closed Systems and Open Minds (Gluckman), 112
Cohn, Bernard, 15, 19–20
Cold War, 14, 18
Collier, Jane, 29
Collier, Stephen, 119
colonialism, 2, 3, 23, 41, 126 n. 15, 126 n. 22, 127 n. 29
Comaroff, Jean, 18, 126 n. 15
Comaroff, John, 18, 126 n. 15
Committee for the Comparative Study of New Nations (University of Chicago), 15, 125 n. 6
complicity, 69, 131 n. 11
Condominas, Georges, 23
Constructing the Field: (Amit), 53
contraption, 71, 74, 77, 81, 92
Crapanzano, Vincent, 26
cultural studies, 16, 31, 103
culture and personality, 2
culture concept, 8, 11, 37, 48, 115–16, 120; culture vs. cultural, 106–11, 133 n. 1 (dialogue vi); holism and, 106–8; identity and, 34–36; material

culture, 38; nature and, 40; semiotics and, 107
Cushman, Richard, 21

Dalí, Salvador, 96
Daston, Lorraine, 39
de Certeau, Michel, 4
deconstruction, 25, 81
Deleuze, Gilles, 4
Delirious New York (Koolhaas), 96
Department of Social Relations (Harvard University), 14–15, 17, 124 n. 2, 125 n. 7
Derrida, Jacques, 4, 17, 25, 41
Dewey, John, 20
Diamond, Stanley, 49, 130 n. 4
Dilthey, Wilhelm, 123 n. 4
Dirks, Nick, 19, 126 n. 22
Dumont, Louis, 19
Durkheim, Émile, 2, 124 n. 2
Dwyer, Kevin, 26

École Normale Supérieure, 119
Eliade, Mircea, 19
elites, 71, 76, 94, 98–99, 113; ordinary people vs., 76–77, 89–91. *See also* experts
Ethnography Through Thick And Thin (Marcus), 79, 124 n. 10, 131 n. 9, 131 nn. 11–12, 132 n. 3 (dialogue v), 132 n. 5 (dialogue v)
eugenics, 56
Europe and the People Without History (Wolf), 29, 127 n. 31
Evans-Pritchard, E. E., 2
evolutionism, 2
exchange, 43, 111
experts, 56, 64, 70–71, 74–76, 78, 108, 113; ordinary people vs., 75–79, 89–91, 109–11. *See also* elites

Fabian, Johannes, 28–29, 128 n. 42
feminism, 26, 29–30, 31, 34, 40, 127
   n. 37, 128 n. 2, 128 n. 46; medical
   anthropology and, 39–40
Ferguson, James, 120
finance, 42, 47, 98, 108–9, 111, 116, 118
First-Time: The Historical Vision of
   an Afro-American People, (Price),
   29
Fischer, Michael M. J., 121
Ford Foundation, 14, 124 n. 2
Fortes, Meyer, 2
Fortun, Kim, 87–89
Foucault, Michel, 4, 17, 19, 26, 41–42,
   47, 51, 61, 88
fragmentation, of the discipline of
   anthropology, 45–47, 52
Frankfurt School, 25
Frazer, James, 2
French DNA (Rabinow), 9, 109, 124
   n. 9, 130 n. 3
French Modern (Rabinow), 69, 132 n. 1
   (dialogue v)
functionalism, 2, 82, 127 n. 39

Gadamer, Hans-Georg, 19, 123 n. 4
Gates, Bill, 56
gay and lesbian studies, 34
Geertz, Clifford, 3–5, 14–16, 18, 19,
   25–28, 40, 124 n. 2, 125 nn. 6–7,
   125 n. 10, 130 n. 5; influence on the
   social sciences, 14–16, 106, 123 n. 4,
   124 n. 1; interpretive anthropology
   and, 2, 3–5, 35, 50, 123 n. 4; thick
   description and, 4, 81, 109, 132 n. 4
   (dialogue v), 133 n. 2
Genealogy of Morals, The (Nietzsche),
   131 n. 6
genomics, 42, 56, 59

globalization, 37, 41–42, 106, 110, 126
   n. 21; modernity as, 108
Godelier, Maurice, 18
Golden Age, of anthropology, 14–15,
   20, 32, 89, 106, 125 n. 5
Gramsci, Antonio, 27
Gupta, Akhil, 120

Habermas, Jürgen, 18, 67, 128 n. 2
Haraway, Donna, 85, 89
Harris, Marvin, 27–28, 31, 127 n. 39
Harvard University, 19–21; Depart-
   ment of Social Relations, 14–15, 17,
   124 n. 2, 125 n. 7
Hegel, G. W. H., 25
Heidegger, Martin, 20
Ho Chi Minh, 23
holism, 35–36, 50, 79, 82, 106–7, 108;
   See also culture concept
Holmes, Douglas, 48
humanitarianism, 41–42, 111
Hunt, Jamer, 96, 132 n. 4 (dialogue vi)
Hutchins, Robert Maynard, 18–19, 126
   n. 18
Hutchins Model. *See* Hutchins, Rob-
   ert Maynard
Hymes, Dell, 22, 24, 28

identity, 5, 29, 33–36, 40, 81, 108, 111
Ilongot Headhunting, 1883–1974
   (R. Rosaldo), 29
"imaginary," 48, 66, 70, 74–78, 131 n. 12
Indonesia, 14
information technology, 97
Institute for Advanced Study
   (Princeton), 16, 125 n. 10
Internet, 56, 84, 109
Interpretation of Cultures, The (Geertz),
   26, 124 n. 1, 132 n. 4, 133 n. 2
interpretive anthropology, 2, 3–5, 15–16

Japan, 15
Johns Hopkins University, 25
journalism, 56–57, 64, 68

Kingdom of Tonga, 21
kinship, 36, 40, 67, 98
Klee, Paul, 113
Koolhaas, Rem, 96
Kuhn, Thomas S., 18, 126 n. 17

Lacan, Jacques, 17
Lakoff, Andrew, 119
Lamphere, Louise, 29
Latour, Bruno, 39, 80–81, 85, 89, 107, 110, 129 n. 8
law, 116, 118
Leacock, Elanor, 26, 127 n. 36
Learning to Labour (Willis), 98
Lee, Benjamin, 40, 128 n. 3
Leenhardt, Maurice, 21
Legitimacy of the Modern Age, The (Blumenberg), 51
Leiris, Michel, 23
Lévi-Strauss, Claude, 2, 19, 27, 126 n. 14
Life Exposed (Petryna), 87–89, 132 n. 7
life sciences, 41–42, 76–78. *See also* genomics; synthetic biology
literary studies, 16
Luhmann, Niklas, 17, 56, 126 n. 12, 131 n. 1

Machine to Make a Future (Rabinow and Dan-Cohen), 8, 50, 76, 130 n. 3
magic, 42–43
Making PCR (Rabinow), 8, 124 n. 8, 130 n. 3
Malinowski, Bronislaw, 2, 7–8, 14, 30, 48, 97, 107, 125 n. 4, 125n. 11, 130 n. 5

Mann, Thomas, 42
Marr, David, 23, 127 n. 29
marxism, 18, 27–28, 30, 127 n. 31, 127 n. 36
Marxism and Literature (Williams), 93–94, 132 n. 1
Massachusetts Institute of Technology, 14–15, 124 nn. 2–3
material culture, 38
McKeon, Richard, 19–20
Mead, Margaret, 35, 61, 125 n. 5
media, 47, 68, 91, 116, 118
media studies, 31
medical anthropology, 39–40
mentorship, 105–6
Miller, Daniel, 38, 129 n. 6
modernism, 50
modernity, 20, 51; the contemporary vs., 57–58; as globalization, 108
Molecular Sciences Institute (University of California, Berkeley), 119
Moore, Barrington, 21
Morgan, Louis Henry, 2
Morganthau, Hans, 19
multi-sited fieldwork/ethnography, 65, 67, 70–71, 73, 75–76, 99, 108–9, 131 n. 11
myth, 42

Nader, Laura, 26, 127 n. 35
nanotechnology, 119
National Center of Excellence for Genomic Sciences, 119
"native point of view," 7, 48, 50, 70, 130 n. 5
Naven (Bateson), 88
Nervous System, The (Taussig), 96
New School, 119

New York Times, 59

Nietzsche, Friedrich, 56, 59, 131 n. 6

non-governmental organizations (NGOs), 41–42, 89

Ockham, William of, 20

Ortner, Sherry, 26–27, 29, 127 n. 37, 128 n. 46

"paraethnography," 48, 70, 116–17, 131 n. 11

paranoia, 96, 132 n. 3

Parsons, Talcott, 14–15, 17, 124 n. 2, 125 n. 9, 126 n. 12

Paul, Robert, 27, 127 n. 40

Peace Corps, 41. *See also* humanitarianism

pedagogy, 10–11, 18–20, 53, 59–60, 64–66, 68–70, 81–84, 86–88, 100–101, 116–21, 124 n. 11

Petryna, Adriana, 87–89, 132 n. 7

Phenomenology of Spirit (Hegel), 25

philology, 3–4, 123 n. 4

philosophy, 4, 123 n. 4; philosophical anthropology, 59

political awareness, 4–5, 20, 22–23, 29. See also *Reinventing Anthropology;* colonialism; postcolonialism

postcolonialism, 30, 40, 41, 66, 126 n. 15, 126 n. 21

postcolonial studies, 31, 42

poststructuralism, 18

Price, Richard, 29

"primitive," the, 16, 27, 29, 31

"problematization," 6, 49, 79, 130 n. 3

Protestant Ethic and the Spirit of Capitalism, The (Weber), 42

Public Culture project, 5, 36–37, 40–42, 128 nn. 2–3

publishing, 86–87, 97, 101–2

Pynchon, Thomas, 96, 132 n. 3 (dialogue vi)

Radcliffe-Brown, A. R., 2

Rapp, Ranya, 29, 78, 129 n. 11

Reflections on Fieldwork in Morocco (Rabinow), 18–19, 24–25, 30

reflexivity, 28, 33, 36, 40, 51, 67–68, 97, 112, 118

Reinventing Anthropology (Hymes), 22, 24, 26, 123 n. 2, 127 n. 27, 127 n. 35, 128 n. 41

religion, 36

representation, 96–97, 112

reproduction, 67; reproductive technology, 39–40, 129 n. 11

resistance, 89

Rheinberger, Hans-Jörg, 39, 129 n. 9

rhetoric, 5, 21–22, 24, 62, 86, 107

Rice University, 9–10, 21, 96, 117–19

Ricœur, Paul, 19

ritual, 36, 42–43, 121

Rosaldo, Michelle, 29, 128 n. 46

Rosaldo, Renato, 29

Sahlins, Marshall, 2, 18, 25–26, 106, 126 n. 14

Said, Edward, 27

Samoa, 61

Sartre, Jean-Paul, 23

Schneider, David, 19–20, 27, 106, 126 n. 20

Scholte, Robert, 28

School of American Research, 127 n. 38

science, 43, 47, 74–75, 78–79, 89, 110–11, 116, 118, 121, 131 n. 8; anthropology as, 18, 63

science and technology studies, 31–32, 39–41, 80, 89, 98, 129 n. 8

science studies. *See* science and technology studies

Segal, Daniel, 120

Silverman, Sydel, 31, 128 n. 47

Social Anthropology, 47

Social Life of Things (Appadurai), 38

social movements, 26, 35, 89, 128 n. 2

South Korea, 108–11

Soviet Union, 30, 36, 56

Strathern, Marilyn, 29, 40, 44, 50, 89, 99, 128 n. 46

Strauss, Leo, 19, 126 n. 23

structural-functionalism, 2, 3, 28

structuralism, 2, 126 n. 14

student-professor relationship. *See* mentorship

subjects: as epistemic partners, 45–46, 65–66, 70, 131 n. 11; reflexive subjects, 90, 112

symbolic anthropology, 2, 15, 126 n. 13

synthetic biology, 58, 119

Taussig, Michael, 96

textuality, 96, 107, 132 n. 6; culture as text, 3–4

thick description, 4, 81, 87, 93, 107, 109, 116, 132 n. 4 (dialogue v)

Things That Talk (Daston), 39

Third World, 27

Time and the Other (Fabian), 29

transnationalism, 94

Trobriand Islanders, 16, 91

Tsing, Anna, 99

Turner, Victor, 2, 18, 126 n. 13

Tylor, Edward Burnett, 2

Ukraine, 87

Universität Tübingen, 1, 6

University of California, Berkeley, 6, 27, 41, 127 n. 35

University of California, Irvine, 117

University of California, San Diego, 119

University of California, Santa Cruz, 27

University of Chicago, 18–20, 27–28, 37, 126 nn. 13–14, 126 n. 18, 126 n. 20, 128 n. 3, 128 n. 42

Untimely Meditations (Nietzsche), 59

Vietnam War, 15, 18, 22–23, 125 n. 5, 126 n. 20, 127 n. 29

Wall Street Journal, 59

wealth, 98–99

Weber, Max, 1, 3, 14–15, 18, 42, 59, 123 n. 4, 124 n. 2

Wenner-Gren Foundation for Anthropological Research, 31, 128 n. 47

White, Hayden, 27

Williams, Raymond, 93–95, 132 n. 1

Willis, Paul, 98, 133 n. 9

Wolf, Eric, 25, 27, 30–31, 106, 127 n. 31

Woodside, Alexander, 23, 127 n. 28

Writing Culture (Clifford and Marcus), 2–6, 9, 25–32, 33, 37–38, 40, 47, 60, 90, 96–99, 101, 112; authority and, 105; background of, 13–14, 21–25, 127 n. 38; feminist response to, 29–30; the humanities and, 16, 26; Leftist response to, 26–27

Yale University, 20, 25

Yanagisako, Sylvia, 29, 120

Zaloom, Caitlin, 42

JAMES D. FAUBION is professor of anthropology at Rice University. He is the author of *Modern Greek Lessons: A Primer in Historical Constructivism* and *The Shadows and Lights of Waco: Millennialism Today*, and editor of the second and third volumes of *The Essential Works of Michel Foucault*. He is currently developing a general analytical framework for the anthropology of ethics.

GEORGE E. MARCUS is Chancellor's Professor at the University of California, Irvine and founder of the Center for Ethnography. His works include *Ethnography through Thick and Thin* and *Anthropology as Cultural Critique* with Michael M. J. Fischer. He was the co-editor of *Writing Culture* with James Clifford, series editor of *Late Editions: Cultural Studies for the End of the Century*, and the founding editor of the journal *Cultural Anthropology*.

PAUL RABINOW is professor of anthropology at the University of California, Berkeley. His works include *Marking Time: On the Anthropology of the Contemporary, Anthropos Today: Reflections on Modern Equipment, Essays on the Anthropology of Reason, Making PCR: A Story of Biotechnology*, and *Michel Foucault: Beyond Structuralism and Hermeneutics* with Hubert Dreyfus. He is the series editor of *The Essential Works of Michel Foucault* and director of human practices for the Synthetic Biology Engineering Research Center (SynBERC).

TOBIAS REES received his Ph.D. in anthropology from the University of California, Berkeley in 2006 and is currently assistant professor in the Departments of Social Studies of Medicine and Anthropology at McGill University. His research focuses on how the recent discovery of adult cerebral plasticity transforms what it means to be neurologically human.

Library of Congress Cataloging-in-Publication Data

Rabinow, Paul.
Designs for an anthropology of the contemporary /
Paul Rabinow and George E. Marcus with James D. Faubion and Tobias Rees.

p. cm.
"A John Hope Franklin Center Book."
Includes bibliographical references and index.
ISBN 978-0-8223-4334-9 (cloth : alk. paper) —
ISBN 978-0-8223-4370-7 (pbk. : alk. paper)
1. Ethnology–Authorship. 2. Ethnology–Research. 3. Ethnology–Methodology.
1. Marcus, George E. 11. Faubion, James D., 1957- 111. Rees, Tobias. 1v. Title.
GN307.7.R34 2008
306–dc22   2008026449